Fathers Matter

Celia Conrad

A guide to contact on separation and divorce

Fathers Matter

2nd Edition (Revised and Expanded)

Celia Conrad

Creative Communications

Dedication

In memory of my beloved father
And for loving fathers everywhere

Published by Creative Communications
Suite 327, 28 Old Brompton Road, London SW7 3SS

Production by Expression, IP23 8HH

ISBN 978 0 9546233 1 9 (0 9546233 1 2)

Further copies of this publication are obtainable from www.fathersmatter.com

Acknowledgments

I would like to thank all the people, who, in speaking to me about their problems, have both encouraged and enabled me to write this book, but who perforce must remain nameless – they know who they are. I would also like to thank everyone who has written to me and/or contacted me with their positive comments about the first edition.

Thanks to Tina and Stephen at Expression for their constructive ideas and speed of production; and to my family for their unstinting encouragement and support. Finally, special thanks to Bob Geldof KBE for his comments on the first edition of this book.

Contents

Comments on the First Edition by Bob Geldof KBE 17

Preface to the Second Edition 18

Preface to the First Edition 19

Introduction 20

Part I Family matters 23

Chapter 1 **The importance of fathers** 23

A father's role 23
How the family unit has changed 23
The contribution a father has to make 24

Maintaining a role 24
Benefits for the children 24
What about cases where the father does not maintain a role? 25

Fathers have feelings too 25
The emotional roller coaster 25
A father's predicament 26
How fathers can help themselves 26
What about when matters become really bad? 27
Help for fathers 27

Chapter 2 **Resolving issues amicably** 28

Reducing conflict 28
The cycle of conflict 28
How the cycle of conflict is compounded 28
Why fathers get caught up in this cycle of conflict 28
Breaking the cycle 29

Seeking assistance from third parties 29
Counselling 29
Purpose 29
Forms of counselling 29
Mediation 30
Definition 30
What the process involves 30
Can a mediator really help with children issues? 30
Not a substitute for legal advice 31

How much does mediation cost and how long does it take? 31
How to find a good mediator 31
Will the children have to attend mediation sessions? 32
Positive benefits of mediation 32
If mediation is beneficial why not make it compulsory? 33
Avoiding the legal process but using the legal advice 33
Clarification of legal position 33
Using the advice constructively 33

Chapter 3 **What about the children?** 34

Telling the children 34
When, where and how 34

How the children might react 34
Relevant factors 34
General reactions 35
General symptoms for children of all ages 35
Reactions at different ages 36
How the parents' relationship impacts on the children's reaction 36

What a father can do to help 36
Put them first 37
Be alert to signs of distress 37

Things a father should not do 37

The children's wishes 38
A child's perspective 38
What are the children thinking? 38
Needs and requirements in light of age and understanding 38

Stepchildren 39
The significance for them of the breakdown of the second relationship 39

Chapter 4 **Post-separation fatherhood** 40

The post split father/child relationship 40
What is going to happen? 40
Carving out a new role 40

Choices for fathers 41
Giving up 41
Hanging in there 41
Reinventing a role for father 41

Making the most of contact: pointers for fathers 42
Make contact as normal as possible 42
Keeping the children entertained 42
Disciplining the children 42
Avoid making any negative comments about their mother 42

Be prepared to give a little 42
Do not pressurize the children 43
Dealing with problems 43
   Reasons for resisting contact 43
   What to do if the children won't see their father 43

External influences: dealing with new partners 44
Adjustments to be made 44
Introducing the children to a new girlfriend 44
The mother's new partner and its relevance to the father/children
  relationship 44
And another thing... 45
Mother moving away 45

Contact with the extended family 46
Grandparents 46
   Contact subject to parental control 46
   Post separation contact 46
   Is promotion of contact generally dependent upon the mother or not? 46
Other family members 47

Chapter 5 **Friend or foe: dealing with your ex** 48

Working together 48
Acting in the children's best interests 48
Facilitating contact 48
   Contact schedules 48

The parental relationship 49

Parental interaction 49

What type of relationship do the parties have? 49
Friends 49
Formal acquaintances 50
Warring parties 50
Sworn enemies 50
Disconnected partnerships 51

Communicate to negotiate 51
It takes two... 51
Communicating effectively 51

Maternal gatekeeping 52
Sabotaging the father/child relationship 52
   What do fathers consider to be sabotage? 52
   Sabotage by mother or justifiable position? 53
   Examples of reasons for maternal sabotage provided by fathers 53
   A mother's justifiable concerns 54
   A final word... 54

Part II The law 55

      Chapter 6   In brief: the law and legal system 55

      The law in outline 55
      The Children Act 1989 55
          Private law orders 55
          Public law orders 56
          Underlying principles under the Children Act 56
      How the court decides 56

      The courts and court protocol 57
      The courts 57
          Jurisdiction 57
          Which courts deal with children matters? 57
          Which is the right court for the case? 57
          Court layout and dress 57
          Relevant court personnel 58
          Court address 58
      Current developments 59
          Working towards a network of Family Court Centres 59
          Court personnel proposals 59
          Creating one simple set of Family Procedure Rules 59

      The role of solicitors and barristers 60

      The court process 60
      General procedure 60
      What is CAFCASS? 61

    Chapter 7 **Your solicitor** 63

      How do I find a good family solicitor? 63
      Personal recommendation 63
      Reputation 63
      Law Society 63
      Resolution (formerly the Solicitors Family Law Association 'SFLA') 64
      Memberships 64
          Collaborative lawyers 64

      Other considerations which may affect the choice of solicitor 65
      How much they cost 65
      Case management 65
      Personal qualities to look out for 66
          Affability 66
          Availability 66
          Ability 66
      Characteristics to avoid 66
          Arrogance 66
          Aggression 66
          Antagonism 67

The solicitor/client relationship 67

Giving and receiving advice 67
    Instructing the solicitor 67
    Seeking clarification 67
    Help to keep the costs down 67

Terms of business and costs 67

The costs letter 67
    Payment of costs 68
    Costs queries 68
    Order for costs & wasted costs orders 68

Public funding 69
    Approved family help 69
    Legal representation 69
    Current developments affecting publicly funded clients 70

Chapter 8 **Getting to grips with the basics** 71

Paternity 71

Starting point 71
    Married fathers 71
    Unmarried fathers 71

Establishing Paternity 72
    Application for a declaration of parentage under the Family Law Act 1986 72
    Obtaining a declaration of parentage unde the Child Support Act s27 72

Proving Paternity by scientific means 72
    Blood samples and DNA Testing 72
    Can I just apply for the court to order a DNA test? 73
    How will the court approach the case? 73
    My ex won't give a sample for DNA testing. What can the court do? 73
    The child's right to know who the biological father is 74
    Can a paternity case be re-opened now that DNA is available? 74

Who's the father now? Altering the legal status 74

Does biology matter? 75

Parental responsibility 76

Meaning 76

Married fathers and parental responsibility 76

Unmarried fathers and parental responsibility 76

Stepfathers and parental responsibility 77
    What are the ways a stepfather can acquire parental responsibility? 77
    Limitations 77

Civil Partners and parental responsibility 78

Is parental responsibility really necessary? 78

Exercising parental responsibility 78

Can a father apply for parental responsibility where his child was not born ithe
  UK and does not reside here? 79

Can a father lose parental responsibility? 79

What happens if the father entrusts his children to the care of someone else? 79
When does parental responsibility come to an end? 79

Chapter 9 **Formalizing arrangements** 81

Child arrangements for divorcing fathers 81
What is meant by the term 'relevant children'? 81
How does the court know if the arrangements proposed are adequate? 81
How will the father find out what arrangements are being proposed? 82
If the judge does not approve the arrangements what will he do? 82
Current developments 82

Child arrangements for unmarried fathers 83

Child arrangements for Civil Partners 83

Deciding whether to make an application to the court 83
Considering the options 83
What are the objectives? 84

Chapter 10 **Preparing your case for court** 86

Automatic right to make an application or not? 86
Those with an automatic right to apply for any s8 order 86
Those with an automatic right to apply for a residence or contact order 86
Those who need leave of the court to apply for a s8 order 86
 Consideration for Grandparents 86

Commencing proceedings 87
Making an application 87
 Completing the application form 87
 What is form C1A? 87
 Tell me about Parenting Plans 88
 Issuing and serving the application 88
Tell me about the proceedings 89
The approach of the court at the First Hearing Dispute Resolution
 Appointment 'FHDRA' 90
 What does investigating the issues mean? 90
 Conciliation 90
 Directions 91
What directions might the court make? 91
 Timetabling the case 91
 Welfare reports 91
 s37 reports 91
 Expert evidence 92
 Witness statements 93
 Limiting disclosure of evidence, reports and documents 93
 The children's attendance 93
 Further hearings and hearing dates 93
The final hearing 94
 Judgment 94

Other procedural concerns... 94
Applying for leave to make a s8 application 94
What does it mean to make an application ex parte? 95
Withdrawing the application 95

What factors will the court consider if an application for a s8 order is made? 96
The welfare principle 96
  The welfare factors 96
The no-order presumption 99
  Where an order would definitely be made 99
Avoidance of delay 99

How long will the order last for? 99

Public law 99
Implications for fathers with children taken into care 99
The local authority has taken the child into care but the father wants contact. Is he entitled? 100
Special guardianship orders 101
Current developments 101

Chapter 11 **Special considerations for specific categories of litigant** 102

Children and s8 proceedings 102
Joining the child as a party 102
Guardians and Next Friends 103
  The child as a party with a guardian or next friend 103
  The child as a party without a guardian/next friend 103
Current developments 104

Litigants in person 104
What is a McKenzie friend? 105
  McKenzie friends and court proceedings 105
  The documents which may be disclosed to a McKenzie friend 106
Other considerations 106

Chapter 12 **Disclosure, Confidentiality & Publicity** 107

When disclosure must be made 107

Rules about what may be disclosed 108
Changes to the rules of disclosure in proceedings held in private 108
  With the court's permission 108
  Where rule 10.20A(3) of the Family Proceedings Rules 1991 (as amended) applies 108
Current developments 109
  Confidence and Confidentiality: Improving Transparency and Privacy in Family Courts 109
  What about anonymity of children in family proceedings? 109
  Experts 110
  Bias 110

Chapter 13 **Residence** 112

The question of residence 112
The primary carer 112
The non-resident father 113
Applying for residence 113
   Considerations for the court 114
Shared residence 114
   The legal position 114
   What fathers want 115
   Attitude of the courts 115

What are the implications of a residence order? 116
Name changes 116
Removing a child from the jurisdiction 118
   Holidays or short periods 118
   Leaving the country permanently 119
   Moving within the jurisdiction 120

Chapter 14 **Contact** 122

Reasonable contact 122
What is reasonable contact? 122
Existing approach 122
The form of contact 123
   Direct contact 123
   Indirect contact 124
   Attaching conditions to contact 125
   What happens where there has been domestic violence? 125
   Interim contact 127
   No contact at all 127
   Varying a court order for contact 128
   Controlling further applications being made 128

Enforcing contact 128
By making an application for a contact order 128
By making an application to enforce the contact order 128
   Children & Adoption Act 2006 128
   Existing powers 129

Chapter 15 **Emergency procedures** 131

Prohibited steps order 131
Where a prohibited steps order would be appropriate 131

Specific issue order 132
Where a specific issue order would be appropriate 132

Child abduction 132
Basics 132
Authorized removal or abduction? 132

Preventative measures 133
  Port alert procedures 133
  Passports 133
Remedies 133
  Convention countries 134
  Non-convention countries 134

Other procedures 134
Missing children – Family Law Reform Act s33 134
Application for recovery of a child – Family Law Reform Act s34 135

Chapter 16 **Appeals** 136

Family Proceedings Court 136
Current developments 136

County Court 136
Appeals 136
Re-hearing or setting aside an order 137

High Court 137

Appeals to the Court of Appeal 137

Orders which may be made 138

Chapter 1 **Other considerations...** 139

Child support 139
The road to hell is paved with good intentions: Child Support Act 1991 139
The existing formula 139
  The rates of pay 139
  Calculation of net income 140
  Shared care 140
Current developments – a new Child Support Regime 141
Contact & Child Support 142

The Human Rights Act 1998 & The Children act 1989 142
Implications of the Human Rights Act for fathers 142
If a father makes an application under the Children Act what effect does the
  Human Rights Act have on the court's decision? 142
Bringing a claim 143
  Can a father bring a claim? 143
  Who are victims and how does a victim bring a claim? 143
  Who can a claim be brought against? 143
Which convention rights affect Family law and fathers' rights? 143
Article 6: the right to a fair trial 143
Article 8: the right to respect for private and family life 144
  Respect for private life 144
  Respect for family life 144
  What would be a justifiable interference into family life? 145

Article 9: freedom of thought, conscience and religion   145
Article 14: prohibition of discrimination   145
Remedies for breach of rights   146
    Changing a decision   146
    Compensation   146
    Declarations of incompatibility   146
Contact & The Human Rights Act   146

Part III Reform 147

Chapter 18 **Pressure for change** 147

Proposals for Reform   147
Consultation papers   147
Giving effect to the intentions of the Children Act 1989   149
Rejecting a legal presumption of equal contact   149
Rejection of bias towards fathers   150

Chapter 19 **A way forward** 151

Contact for 'fit' parents   151

Other jurisdictions – lessons to be learned?   151

Rights for the children   152

Final thoughts   153

Appendix **Some useful contacts and addresses** 155

Comments on the First Edition by Bob Geldof KBE

I wish this book had been around when I went through my contemptible experiences at the hands of the Family Courts. It would have helped explain what was happening to me. It could have been the clear, cool voice of knowledge, experience, understanding and sympathy that is necessary to take men through the grief and pain and loss of having their children taken from them simply on the basis of their being male – a very suspect condition if you're a father, at least in the blinkered, myopic, outdated and reactionary view of our legal hierarchy.

This book is a timely, invaluable guide around the many hurdles and obstructions the Courts will put in a man's way to stop him being a dad to his kids. Read it and learn. Then try and change things so that children may know their dad loves them even if the law does not.

Bob Geldof KBE, July 2004

Preface to the Second Edition

Since the first edition was published in October 2003 there have been a number of developments in this area of family law. The law is increasingly having to expand and adapt to the different circumstances which may arise when parties separate and/or divorce to take account of the variety of 'family' relationships within our changing society. This is reflected in the introduction of both the Adoption & Children Act 2002 and the Civil Partnership Act 2004. A civil partner in a registered partnership is now able to acquire parental responsibility of his/her partner's child in the same way as a step-parent – thus giving rights to single sex-partners. Gay and lesbian parents may adopt under the Adoption & Children Act 2002. Lesbian couples may have a child by donor insemination.

Of course relationships where one or either party already has children from one or more previous relationships are hardly new, but there is an increasing number of cases where the party applying for an order under the Children Act 1989 has no biological connection with the child or children who happen to be the subject of that application.

The difficulties of promoting, facilitating and enforcing contact between children and parents who do not live with them are ongoing. The Children & Adoption Act 2006 includes new measures to deal with this and we consider them in Part II. Over the past few years the Department of Constitutional Affairs (DCA), which replaced the Lord Chancellor's Department in June 2003, has produced a number of consultation papers to address key reforms in this area in response to direct criticisms of the family court system and mounting pressure for change from campaigners both within and outside the legal system.

In 2004 the DCA produced a Green Paper *Parental Separation: Children's Needs & Responsibilities* setting out its agenda for reform, following which the Constitutional Affairs Committee carried out an inquiry *Family Justice: the operation of the Family Courts* to consider the Government's proposals and to seek submissions from interested parties on the proposals. I myself submitted written evidence and attended one of the oral evidence sessions in January 2005 together with Tony Coe, the President of Equal Parenting Council and John Baker of Families need Fathers.

Following the enquiry the Government produced its report *Next Steps* setting out its agenda. We look at the reforms and proposed changes where appropriate throughout the course of this book. In Part III we review the whole issue of reform and contentious matters such as compulsory mediation and a statutory presumption of shared care.

As well as completely revising the first edition, this second edition has been expanded to include additional sections on paternity; civil partnerships; grandparents; the separate representation of children; litigants in person; disclosure, confidentiality and publicity; and appeals. Mindful that there has been important case law over recent years, I have included the case reference details for cases which might be of further interest. Finally, as before, there is an appendix of some useful contacts and addresses at the back of the book.

Celia Conrad, February 2007

Preface to the First Edition

The idea for this book was conceived as long ago as 1999, while I was still working full time in private practice. One father, for whom my then firm was acting, asked me if I had considered writing a book to help address fathers' issues. After a chance encounter with a father in my local gym – my firm had ironically represented the mother – and to whom I subsequently spoke at length about his own predicament, I felt compelled to write this book.

The first draft was completed over two years ago at a time when, unfortunately, the whole issue of fathers' rights was still regarded by many as only a passing phase and I was told that there would be no interest in a book solely directed at fathers, as it would be too narrow and too controversial. This perception has persisted despite the fact that during this period of time there has been ever increasing media interest in the plight of fathers. Rarely a week has gone by without us reading or hearing about harrowing cases of fathers who have fought for but lost contact with their children, some of whom have been financially crippled in the process.

Frustrated by the lack of cohesion in this area and progress on their behalf, fathers' rights groups have been driven to take on the campaign for change themselves. This is no more evident than in the activities of Fathers4Justice, a civil rights group launched in December 2002 to support estranged fathers, which has gained enormous media coverage and aims to raise the public's awareness of the injustices fathers suffer and is pressing for change within the law.

The recent criticisms by fathers' rights groups of the judiciary, has sparked considerable debate. Are the courts biased towards fathers? Certainly, the majority of fathers who have been through the court process have no faith in it to produce an unbiased result. Their confidence in the legal system has already been undermined. A father is not interested in hearing his lawyer say to him at the end of a case, after he has expended thousands and thousands of pounds, that the result is very unfair and the legislation needs to be changed but there is nothing he can do about it because that is the law. This is not going to resolve the problem for the father and is regarded by many as 'a cop out' and does none other than to inflame an already heated situation.

Celia Conrad , October 2003

Introduction

The content of this book stemmed from a number of conversations I had with male clients during the course of their relationship break-up and in relation to their respective roles as fathers. Several clients told me that, on separating from their wives/partners, they searched the bookshelves in their public library and all the major bookstores in order to find some information for fathers going through a divorce, or who were 'splitting up' with their partner. The only guides they could find were for mothers.

Essentially what they were looking for was a user-friendly guide, which provided a thorough overview of the issues they now faced and addressed ways of dealing with those issues constructively. They indicated to me that they needed a comprehensive guide dealing with both the emotional impact on and legal implications of separation and divorce for fathers and their children. Although there were DIY divorce guides and books on child law, there were no specific guides relating to fathers' problems from a father's perspective. That is, to assist fathers with any queries, worries, and emotions – as well as the general confusion surrounding a divorce/relationship breakdown. Additionally, they wanted to have a better understanding of their legal position and the legal process as applicable to them. In short they wanted a practical handbook for fathers.

I have written this book for all loving fathers who wish to build and/or maintain healthy relationships with their children after separation and divorce. I hope that by reading this book they will be able to cope better with the breakdown of their relationship and the adjustments that have to be made by them and their children upon separation. The breakdown of any relationship is traumatic and a degree of anger and conflict between parties is likely at this time. But when a relationship comes to an end, and especially in the early stages when emotions are riding high, understandably the parties often cannot see the bigger picture and the bearing that the actions of today will have upon their relations tomorrow, and the impact this will have upon their children because it is clouded by an emotional haze. It is evident that how parties interact, and what steps they take to reduce conflict and to resolve the issues between them, not only has a major bearing on their future relationship but also on their children and in turn that relationship. Both parents need to work together for the benefit of their children and to act in their children's best interests. This is crucial.

A father who has been able to reach an amicable agreement with the mother probably does not need to read this book. This book is directed at fathers who want to reach an agreement with the mother of their children but for one reason or another cannot do so. Clearly it is preferable, and ultimately in the interests of all parties concerned, to avoid court proceedings; but the reality is that for many a father reaching an agreement with the mother is like reaching for the moon. There may be some cases where all that is required is intervention from an independent third party to guide, direct and assist the parents, to enable them to work through the issues so as to enable them to forge an agreement acceptable to them. Both parents have to be fully committed to resolving the problem, and to finding a workable solution. But this is where the problems arise, as a lack of cohesion and compromise between the parties is generally one of the major stumbling blocks to reaching an agreement.

Independent third parties include counsellors, doctors, mediators and lawyers. Counsellors may be able to help with the emotional aspects; doctors with the symptoms of trauma and stress; mediators with clarification of the issues and assistance in putting them into perspective. A family lawyer has many hats. To a client on an emotional roller coaster, in the initial stages of a divorce or potentially heavily contested child application, a client may use their lawyer as a confidante, counsellor, emotional prop, punch bag, sounding board, listening post, psychologist, as well as advisor.

Seeking the advice of a lawyer over a child issue does not mean proceedings must be commenced or at least not immediately – unless there is an imminent threat of danger to the child or the possibility that he/she might be abducted. In this situation court proceedings will be the first resort, on the basis that urgent action is required, since delay could be detrimental to the child. But if a father is in any doubt as to his legal position he should seek legal advice as knowledge of the legalities of a particular situation may assist in dealings with the mother. The role of a lawyer, as advisor, is to advise clearly and constructively so that rash decisions which a party might later come to regret when the consequences of those decisions come full circle are avoided. Unfortunately a complaint by many clients, male or female, is that it is the lawyers who all too often inflame the situation and are confrontational, aggressive, and litigious and add fuel to the flames. This in turn creates more conflict and is destructive.

Many of the fathers I have spoken to, who have taken legal action, told me that they did so reluctantly. The reality of the situation is that, although ideally they wanted to resolve questions relating to their children and avoid conflict, court applications and costs, they felt they had no other alternative as the contact arrangements proposed by the mother, or already in existence, were totally unacceptable to them. In some cases communication had broken down completely between the parties, or if they were still talking to each other they could not do so without arguing, and/or they were entrenched in their respective position.

Compared with the number of children involved, the number of cases that reach a final court hearing is small because the majority of cases are compromised along the way. However, this does not mean that fathers are satisfied with the compromise reached and that they are 'getting a fair deal' from the legal system. In fact most of the fathers I have dealt with did not think they had been well served and been 'squeezed' by it. A case might be compromised, for example, where a father wishes to protect his children from the 'fall out' of the proceedings and the adverse affect a court case may have on them, or where he gives up after receiving legal advice that his chances of success are next to nothing. Therefore the fact that a matter is compromised is definitely not an indication of a positive outcome for either the father or his children.

The Children Act 1989 assumes that the parties will do their best to resolve differences by negotiation and cooperation. It introduced a non-intervention and no-order policy. This means that the court will only intervene and make an order where it would be better to make an order than no order at all. This is ironic. The fact is the law only works for parents who are able to act in the best interests of their children and reach an amicable agreement, because in that situation the law does not need to intervene at all. The problem arises when parents cannot agree and the law is used to try to resolve what they cannot. Reliance upon the legal system to deliver what fathers want has left them bitterly disappointed. Unfortunately for a father, resorting to legal proceedings rarely achieves the desired result.

I did not write this book because I am pro fathers and anti mothers, but to highlight the areas of concern fathers expressly requested I address, to provide the information they need and to help raise their profile. In fact much of the material in this book is of relevance to both parents and anyone connected to a party in this situation, not just fathers.

Chapter 1
The importance of fathers

A father's role

The concept of the family, and the role of a father within it, has been defined and redefined over the centuries. Traditionally it was expected and accepted that the male's role, as husband and father, was to go out to work and to provide financially for the family. The female's role, as wife and mother, was to run the home and care for the children and to be the emotional crutch of the family. By virtue of the fact that fathers were the breadwinners, and not at home with their children, their financial contribution was regarded as more important than their emotional one. A mother's relationship is 'seen' to be closer and it has been assumed that women, by nature, are better suited to love and care for the children.

However, more women now have their own careers and therefore contribute financially to the family, sometimes equally or even more. The number of situations where fathers share the parenting duties with the mother has steadily increased. Where the father is self-employed and able to work around any child care arrangements he may even be the primary carer. This social change has been recognized; shared residence orders are made far more frequently by the courts than they were a decade ago when they were rare and only made in unusual circumstances. We examine this shift towards shared residence orders in detail in Chapter 13.

How the family unit has changed

That 'traditional' concept of the family has completely changed. The stereotypical division of a mother and father's roles does not match the reality of the modern family. In today's society many parties do not marry, almost four out of ten children are born to cohabiting couples and there are more single mothers where no father is present at all. National Statistics reveal that in 2004 nearly nine out of ten lone parents were lone mothers and in Spring 2005 nearly one in four children lived in a lone-parent family. In 2001 ten percent of all families with dependent children in the UK were step-families. There are more families where both parents or one parent and his/her partner are of the same sex.

The definition of what constitutes a family unit is now very wide, but what is clear from the statistics is that some children will live in more than one family unit during their childhood without a father figure at all.

The contribution a father has to make

What is a father's contribution to contemporary family life supposed to be? There has been a shift on the financial front so you might expect that this would mean a shift on the emotional front in favour of fathers. The reality is that from an emotional point of view mothers are regarded differently from fathers and there is definitely a lack of agreement about a father's potential role in child-rearing. Mother Nature is a major factor and the maternal bond is a very strong and special bond, but this does not mean that a father loves his child any less than a mother does or is incapable of loving his child as much.

There is no question that a father plays a pivotal role in his children's lives, and they in his. In fact, in 1998 the Government produced a consultation paper *Supporting Families* in which it was stated that fathers do have a crucial role to play in their children's upbringing. Fathers have a very positive contribution to make to their families both emotionally and financially. This role is no less important than the one mothers play, albeit the role is played out differently. A mother and father each have a significant contribution to make. They have different styles of parenting and different attributes and should complement one another. Parenthood should be a partnership.

So to what extent does all of this impact on a father's role with his child after a relationship split? How does this affect his role?

Maintaining a role

Benefits for the children

The fact that a loving father no longer lives with his children does not make him any less significant, nor does it mean he wishes to be uninvolved with them. In the majority of cases this could not be further from the truth. A devoted father strives to have contact with his children and to retain a strong and positive presence in their lives. It is only circumstances that have dictated that he no longer lives with them. A father who does not live with his children is known as the 'non-resident' parent, a term which in itself is a bone of contention for fathers.

These fathers feel they provide the important function of 'being there' for their children. Many do this by helping with homework, attending parents' evenings at school and taking children to and from school. They can offer an alternative home when the need arises. They usually provide an important base for their children and relish taking responsibility for them, which they may not have had until they have sole care of them.

Certainly it is easier for a father to build a strong relationship with his children where there is a harmonious relationship between the parents, but that does not mean that a father who has to overcome obstacles cannot maintain a role, although it is considerably harder.

What about cases where the father does not maintain a role?

Where does this leave the children of one parent families or where fathers do not wish to be involved? Are we to believe that these children will not be as well-adjusted because they are denied that relationship? Many single parents will argue that this is not the case, and their children go on to do well at school and to form healthy relationships. Most of these children will have never known a father's presence. That may not be detrimental but it certainly does not mean that they would not have benefited from it.

It is of course a sad fact that not all fathers wish to have contact with their children. We hear complaints from fathers about mothers who do their best to frustrate contact but equally there are fathers who do not behave in a responsible manner. There are cases where a father who, despite repeated pleadings from the mother for him to visit, or even applications by the mother to the court for an order for him to have contact, still neglects his children.

The father may have left his partner for someone else or just disappeared at the end of the relationship and ceased to have contact with his children and then, after several years, decides he wishes to re-establish contact and wonders why the mother does not play ball. It is not surprising that in these circumstances a mother protests and is hostile if a father turns up demanding extensive contact and threatening her with court applications if she does not comply. On the other hand, for fathers who are consistent in their intentions and behave in a responsible manner towards their children there is no reason why contact should be denied. Cases of errant fathers must not be allowed to prejudice the cases of those fathers who are genuine.

We look in detail at fathers' post-separation relationship with their children in Chapter 4.

Fathers have feelings too

The emotional roller coaster

Fathers say that being separated from their children has a devastating effect on them. When they no longer see their children every day and/or their contact is limited or even prevented, they suffer a terrible sense of 'loss' and can feel helpless. Anyone who has lost someone very close to them only has to put themselves into a father's position and imagine his feelings in such circumstances. Men of course are not meant to be emotional – big men never cry. But they are and they do. Fathers are not immune to the emotional roller coaster. The emotions that emerge can come and go unpredictably, and they can feel up and then down and as if everything is out of control. They may experience feelings of grief, sadness, misery, desperation, desolation, isolation, rage, resentment, bitterness and hostility too. Sometimes the emotions are so overwhelming that fathers have suicidal thoughts. Sometimes they act on them.

I have seen fathers in a terrible emotional state and who have broken down in tears on the telephone, trying to come to terms with their situation. Numerous fathers have told me how heartbroken they were because they could not see their children every day. For fathers who are devoted to their children being separated from them is unbearable. A client who was a successful businessman said that the toughest decision he had ever had to make was in relation to his children. He felt emotional all the time but he was afraid of showing his true feelings because he believed it would be seen as a sign of weakness in the negotiations. It was not surprising he was feeling emotional because he genuinely loved his children and was upset about the effect the divorce was having on them. The point is fathers have feelings too.

A father's predicament

Fathers find themselves in a no-win situation. They do not think the legal system addresses these points and that it has little regard for how they feel when decisions are made relating to their children. Right or wrong that is the perception. Unable to reach an agreement with the mother and faced with battling against the establishment it is no surprise that these fathers are under emotional stress. One father told me there were times when he felt like walking off the roof because he felt so desperate about his situation but the one thing which would always stop him taking that step was his love for his daughter.

A father often feels pushed right to the limit; desperate times may mean desperate measures. Some fathers take drastic action. Some fathers are so terrified of losing their children that they abduct them. While such action can never be condoned, there is a world of difference between a desperate father who just wants to spend time with his children and is driven to snatching them because he has not had any meaningful contact for months, and a father who abducts with malicious motive, who wants to punish the mother by taking her children away from her permanently and/or who poses a serious danger to the children.

There are some terrible cases where children have been abducted to a country with which the United Kingdom does not have a reciprocal agreement in respect of the abduction and return of children. These are known as non-convention countries as they do not comply with the Hague Convention which provides procedures for tracing children and their return. In any event, the consequences for a father who abducts are dire, because, if he is caught, he will have ruined any chances of meaningful contact with his child. This will be the case whatever the reason and ultimately it is the children who suffer the most. The issue of child abduction is addressed more fully in Chapter 15.

How fathers can help themselves

As matters progress, feelings change and the issues or challenges faced are also different. There are things a father can do to make it through:

- Look after himself. It helps to cope with the changes going on around him. Eating and sleeping are important. At times of stress people do not/cannot/ forget to eat and have difficulty sleeping.
- Keep focused on what the objectives are but be realistic.
- Take a step back and think about the implications of any actions taken and avoid making decisions that he will later regret. Revenge tactics may seem a good idea at the time but often backfire and do not bring about desired results.

- Talk about his problems to someone he can trust if he can. It does not change things but it may make him feel better because holding emotions inside can exacerbate stress and illness.
- Take time out for himself. With so many changes going on in his life at this time he is likely to feel overloaded.
- Consider writing down his feelings. Some fathers keep diaries to vent their frustrations.

One of the questions fathers ask is how they are meant to feel. There probably is no right answer. We are all individuals and one father may react differently from another. It also depends upon the particular circumstances. However, the range of emotions referred to above is indicative of a father's reaction in the majority of cases.

What about when matters become really bad?

It is common for people going through emotional trauma to feel depressed and have problems concentrating on work and focusing on anything else, because nothing else matters. Many fathers who run their own businesses report a major downward turn in productivity, as they cannot focus due to the surrounding uncertainty. They are unable to commit time to the business because they are devoting so much time to personal matters. Many fathers in employment find it difficult to hold down their jobs when their emotional life is in chaos. On the other hand, some fathers bury themselves in their work as a means of dealing with the fact that their family has fallen apart.

One father told me that he found it very difficult to cope when he could not see his children. He became an emotional wreck. He had been taking sleeping tablets and anti-depressants and became dependent on them. He developed severe depression and was withdrawn. Fortunately, his family saw the warning signs and encouraged him to seek professional help. The support of his family and the qualified professionals helped him through. Others are not so lucky. They do not have that emotional support. Alone and depressed they become dependent on medications, other drugs or alcohol and unable to function without them. Sometimes it is all too much and the dreadful reality is that there are cases where fathers have committed suicide because they have not been allowed to see their children. The tragedy is that, on the face of it, these were fathers who appeared to be 'coping'. Recently I was contacted by a grandmother whose son set fire to himself because he had been refused contact for nearly two years with his not yet three year old daughter. We rarely hear of these terrible cases though and this is an issue that must be addressed.

Help for fathers

There is an ever increasing number of organizations which provide information and support to fathers and actively campaign for fathers' rights. For any father encountering problems in relation to contact, or who needs general support and guidance, these organizations are well worth contacting because they offer a wealth of information for fathers. There are numerous websites directed at father-related matters. I have included details of where to find them in the Appendix.

Chapter 2
Resolving issues amicably

Reducing conflict

How can parents resolve issues in relation to their children when they are at loggerheads? In the introduction we looked briefly at how they deal with conflict and handle their relationship and why this has a major bearing on the way they resolve issues generally, including matters relating to their children. We now examine this more closely. We consider the on-going parental relationship in Chapter 4.

The cycle of conflict

In any relationship each person is constantly reacting to the other. We may not think about this consciously but this is what happens. If someone is judgmental and critical towards a person how he/she reacts will be very different from how he/she reacts if someone is pleasant and full of praise for him/her. In the first instance he/she is more likely to respond well to the person, unless he/she has reason to suspect that there is a hidden agenda behind the display of warmth. Either way what is happening is that each person is determining the other's reaction. Put this in the divorce/relationship breakdown/contact context where there is an explosion of emotions, when parties are most likely to be feeling anger, hurt, guilt, regret, hate, fear and lash out at the other party. What happens then? It creates conflict.

How the cycle of conflict is compounded
Sometimes we feel that the only way to resolve something in our favour is to fight for it. If we fight enough we will achieve the desired result, so we believe, and the other party will back down. That may happen sometimes but generally what happens is the opposite. The more we fight someone the more of a threat we become to them and they fight back harder, and this in turn comes back on to us; there is a cycle of conflict. This is all too apparent in the father versus mother context.

Why fathers get caught up in this cycle of conflict
I asked a number of fathers why they fought so hard for contact. The answer was unequivocal: fear of losing the children. The problem that many fathers have is that on separation they are invariably the ones to leave the family home so they immediately lose continuity of contact with their children. A father does not start on an equal footing with a mother. He is on the back foot.

If the child is an infant then the contact is more likely to be limited, as generally he/she will stay with the mother unless the mother has a particularly good arrangement with the father and allows the child to stay with him. If the father moves into rented accommodation, it may be unsuitable for the children to stay there and other less satisfactory arrangements may have to be made.

Sometimes this means that a father will be unable to have as much contact as he would like with his children and, with relations in the family already strained as a result of the breakup, contact may be difficult. Fathers also fear about precedents for contact being set at these early stages. An agreement may not be possible and many fathers complain that they find it extremely difficult, next to impossible, to establish any regular pattern of contact with their children, so naturally they fight for it.

If fathers were guaranteed satisfactory contact then the fear of losing the children would evaporate and so would the need to fight for it. We look at the current legal position in Chapter 14. We know that court proceedings should be seen as a method of last resort and that parties should look for an amicable solution. If court proceedings are issued they are generally resolved in some sort of compromise which nobody finds satisfactory; the final solution ordered by a court could even be less satisfactory. But what are the alternatives for a father who has not seen his children for months or even years due to the recalcitrance of the mother?

Breaking the cycle

In order to agree, parties need to communicate, but if communication breaks down and barriers go up that becomes a remote possibility, particularly when every attempt to communicate turns into an argument. The ideal situation would be to take a step back from the other person and let matters calm down, not to enter into tit-for-tat arguments and focus on ending the conflict for the sake of the children. In reality, in such an emotionally charged situation where both parties are entrenched in their positions, the likelihood of achieving this is minimal.

Seeking assistance from third parties

Sometimes third party intervention can help but clearly it will not do so unless both parties are truly committed to the welfare of their children.

Counselling

Purpose

The purpose of counselling is to help the parties deal with the emotional side of their relationship. A party might attend counselling sessions for a number of reasons and those reasons vary from individual to individual.

Forms of counselling

There are different forms of counselling and different purposes for it. A father might want to find out if he can salvage his relationship and how he might do that. If his relationship cannot be saved then counselling may help him cope with his feelings, and to come to terms with the situation. After separation he may seek counselling to enable him to deal with all the changes that are happening in his personal life. This includes the adjustments that have been enforced upon him in terms of his relationships with his ex, his children and any new partners on both sides. He may also want help in dealing with issues raised by other members of his family.

When people think of marriage guidance they think of Relate. Relate does not just provide Marriage Guidance Services but an extensive range of counselling services. It has offices in most areas. Organizations such as the Institute of Family Therapy, National Marriage Guidance, Jewish Marriage Council and Catholic Marriage Advisory Council provide counselling.

Mediation

Definition
If parties feel they cannot negotiate themselves but still wish to, then they can attend mediation sessions. Mediation is not Marriage Guidance. It is not counselling. Originally the mediation process in the UK was called conciliation but the word mediation is now universally used (probably because conciliation could be confused with reconciliation, and that is not what mediation is for). In mediation it is assumed the marriage has broken down and the focus is on helping the parties resolve the issues between them arising out of separation and this includes their children.

What the process involves
Mediation is a process open to a couple, married or unmarried, and the aim of it is to assist the parties to work though the issues between them with a view to reaching a compromise. It does not matter whether they are legally represented or not, nor whether they have started any legal proceedings. In mediation both parties agree to the appointment of a neutral third party who is impartial and who has no 'authority' to make any decisions in respect of their issues. In other words, unlike a court that will make a decision binding upon them, the mediator as a neutral individual is there to help them work through their problems. This is the case whether it is in relation to separation, divorce, children issues, property and finances or any other issues that may be raised. The mediator's role is to help the parties to reach their own informed decisions by negotiation and without adjudication.

In mediation the parties control the decision-making. The mediator cannot bind them to any decision, but is there to chair the meetings, manage and control the process, and guide them through the issues.

Can a mediator really help with children issues?
As well as dealing with 'all issues' mediation, there is also child-focused mediation. Mediation is a popular way to try and sort out contact problems. The mediators who work in this area may have experience as counsellors, social workers, family therapists or family solicitors.

If the mediation is child-focused the parties will concentrate on the children issues. They can discuss arrangements for the children, with whom they are to live, and how much time they should be spending with each parent, or whether they are to be looked after by another relative. A mediator can look at schooling and religion and encourage the parents to come to an agreement in relation to these points as well. It may well be that the parents are poles apart on these issues, and in particular on the 'living' arrangements for the children, but if nothing else a mediator might be able to help with interim arrangements.

Not a substitute for legal advice

Mediation may be a way of avoiding litigation but it is not a substitute for taking independent legal advice. Parties may want to take advice about what they discussed at the mediation. At the same time, there is no point in going along to mediation sessions if they do not go there with an open mind and are not prepared to tackle the issues between them. They will be wasting everybody's time including their own. If parties have legal advisors they should keep them fully informed of any progress made, as any legal action to be taken may depend upon the outcome of the mediation.

How much does mediation cost and how long does it take?

Mediation sessions are normally one and a half hours each. When giving advice solicitors generally charge by the hour, so if they are mediators they will generally charge their hourly rate. Some mediators operate a sliding scale of fees and the amount paid depends upon how much a party can afford, depending upon his/her income. There are some voluntary organizations as well. If a party has virtually no money he/she may be entitled to public funding through the Community Legal Service (CLS). CLS replaced the Legal Aid Board and has a scheme for funding mediation. (We look at the cost of funding legal costs and the role of the CLS in Chapter 7.) The number of sessions will depend on the issues, but five or six sessions are not uncommon.

How to find a good mediator

If parties are going to proceed with mediation then they need to find a properly qualified mediator otherwise they cannot hope to derive any benefit from it. This is essential as only a properly trained and accredited mediator can provide a quality and meaningful service for them.

To find a mediator a party could contact, among other organizations:

- The UK College of Family Mediators. This is the professional body for all family mediators in England, Scotland, Wales and Northern Ireland.
- National Family Mediation, NFM, is a registered charity and offers 'not for profit' family mediation services to couples in England and Wales. NFM is a Founder Body of the UK College of Family Mediators.
- Resolution's (formerly The Solicitors Family Law Association) mediators are solicitors specializing in family law who have trained to be mediators. From January 2002 Resolution members who have been trained by other recognized bodies and have the necessary experience may apply to be Resolution mediators. They will have to attend a familiarization programme. As solicitors they have an in depth knowledge of the legal process and may be able to assist the parties to make fair and sensible arrangements both in relation to their finances and children. Alternatively, they may prefer an independent

mediator totally removed from the legal process. At the end of the day it is up to the parties.

- The Law Society is the regulatory body, governing solicitors. It has produced a Family Mediation Code of Practice. The Code is addressed to solicitors who practise as mediators in family disputes. It has a specific section dealing with families and children.
- Family Mediation Helpline. This was launched by the Government in May 2006. The helpline is available by calling 0845 60 26 627 or visiting www.familymediation.co.uk The helpline is manned by trained staff who will provide general information on family mediation and its suitability for particular cases and then put couples in touch with family mediators in their area.

Will the children have to attend mediation sessions?

The Law Society Family Mediation Code of Practice sets out specific guidelines for this. In all cases where children are involved the mediator should have regard to their needs and interests. The law provides that a mediator should have arrangements designed to ensure that both parents are encouraged to consider 'whether and to what extent each child could be given the opportunity to express his or her wishes in the mediation.'

The mediator should consider whether and when the children may be directly involved in mediation. The mediator should not ordinarily invite children to be directly involved unless specifically trained to do so and alive to issues such as confidentiality and the dynamics inherent in doing so. This is in accordance with the code.

It is extremely important that a mediator who wants to involve children in the mediation process should undertake specific training covering these issues.

Positive benefits of mediation

This is a 'conflict resolution' process, so in other words it is a means by which parties address and agree the issues between them and therefore avoid contested court proceedings. Even if they do not resolve all their issues, the fact that they have attempted to mediate is positive.

Mediation promotes co-operation between the parties, and looks at both their needs in the round rather than just one side, so compromise is more likely. Furthermore, it creates options other than winning and losing which is generally how parties will perceive their case once the court battle lines are drawn up.

Because each party has a say in the mediated agreement, it tends to include more specific details and actually reflects both their wishes, whereas if the matter proceeds to court there will be an enforced result and sometimes neither party will achieve what was hoped for. A mediated agreement may subsequently form the basis of an agreed order to be submitted to the court, that is, a consent order.

However, the subject matter of any negotiations forming part of the mediation process is 'privileged from disclosure in subsequent court proceedings'. During the course of mediation sessions parties may discuss contact arrangements, but ultimately fail to come to an overall agreement and one party may decide to make an application to the court for a contact order. A party would not be able, within the context of those proceedings, to refer to what had been 'discussed' at the mediation sessions. This is the same in terms of any other negotiations that take place with a view to settlement, more commonly known as 'without prejudice negotiations'. This is important because if parties were afraid that anything they said could be used against them by the other party, they would never negotiate. Matters discussed in the mediation session are confidential except when a criminal offence is disclosed.

Mediation is thus a way of encouraging the parties to compromise and agree without putting them under pressure. It does not mean though that if parties do not manage to dot all the 'I's and cross all the 'T's at the mediation session that either of them should decide to change their position completely just to be awkward. It is not constructive, although it has been known to happen.

If mediation is beneficial why not make it compulsory?

There is no obligation on privately paying divorcing couples with children to attend mediation. This is in direct contrast with divorcing couples with children who need public funding – they will be refused legal aid unless they attend mediation. That being said, there is nothing to stop a legally-aided party who has no intention of settling from attending mediation, saying it has failed and then proceeding to court anyway.

As a result of the Children & Adoption Act 2006 which we look at in detail in Chapter 14, the court will have the power to direct a party to attend an information session about a mediation session but not a mediation session itself. There is considerable debate about whether mediation should be compulsory or not. An argument against making it so is that it is supposed to be a voluntary process and it defeats the purpose of it if couples are required to attend compulsorily. It is also considered unsuitable where there is domestic violence or abuse.

Avoiding the legal process but using the legal advice

Clarification of legal position

If a father is divorcing or separating then it is likely he will be taking legal advice in relation to that as well as financial matters, and this will include maintenance for the children, where they are to live and their schooling. The children are likely to be at the forefront of any dealings with his solicitor.

Using the advice constructively

Ideally the advice given should be used to help resolve the issues with the mother. Focusing on finding solutions which are positive to everybody is the key to resolving issues without conflict. The difference between the parties resolving conflict themselves and an adversarial position, is that the former focuses on the need to find a solution and the latter on winning. At least that is how it is perceived. To the extent that they can do that, the legal process becomes redundant and costs are reduced. But again this is an ideal situation and many parties never reach this stage because either or both of them simply have no intention of meeting the other half way.

We will look at the choice of solicitor in Part II.

Chapter 3
What about the children?

Telling the children

When parents separate and the father leaves, a child's world is turned completely upside down. Everything changes and the established pattern of life no longer exists. Children are faced with an abrupt change in their lives, especially so if their father suddenly leaves without warning and they had no idea that there were any problems at home. It affects their sense of security.

When, where and how

Children should be kept informed about what is happening between their parents as, after all, the changes are affecting them too and more than may be apparent. How, when and where they are told about the divorce and what they are told and understand can have a significant effect on their reaction. The way this is done can either reduce or increase their worries and fears.

All of this depends upon a number of factors including their age and understanding. How a child aged three is told that 'daddy has left' will be different from telling a child aged thirteen; all children are different. They will have views, issues and wishes too. The way they convey them will depend upon their age and understanding.

Timing is of the essence. Parents do not want to break the news to the children suddenly but they must not delay for too long either. If the decision to separate is final then parents must make that clear, because otherwise the children may pursue a false hope that their parents will be reunited. Parents should tell their children jointly if that is possible. The children need to be assured at all times that they are loved. They need to be told this on an ongoing basis and shown that they will be loved whatever happens.

The children may worry about any changes. Parents need to be specific and realistic about practical changes in their children's lives. They may be changing home, school, having to make new friends. If either parent has a new partner then they will have to deal with that new relationship too.

How the children might react

Relevant factors

It is very difficult to be exact about the impact of divorce/separation on a specific child although there has been much research into children's different reactions and there are a number of factors to consider:

- Their age and ability to understand, express and explain what they feel. Children's cognitive development varies.
- Gender. Girls react better than boys do apparently!
- Their nature.
- Their parents' relationship.
- Social background.

General reactions

Children may:

- Feel a terrible loss and miss the daily presence of their father in their life.
- Convince themselves that 'this is not happening' and go into a state of denial.
- Think that if they shut out the problem then it will simply go away.
- Feel very angry and lash out at the father for leaving them, believing that he has betrayed them and has 'broken' up the family.
- Become withdrawn and introvert.
- Believe that they have in some way contributed to the 'break up' and feel it is their fault that their father has left because he no longer loves them as a result of something they have done.

When children realize that the situation is not going to change, despite anything they say or do, they can become very depressed. Parents need to look out for behavioural and emotional changes in their children at this time. Depression is apparently one of the most common psychological/psychiatric disorders and children are not immune, particularly when their parents separate. Feeling sad or depressed is a normal reaction to a tragedy, change or a significant loss.

General symptoms for children of all ages

These symptoms vary from child to child. Some may display many symptoms and others only one or two. Here are examples to look out for, some of which have been provided by former clients. Once again this list is not exhaustive:

- Crying, feeling sad, helpless or hopeless.
- Feeling discouraged or worthless.
- Loss of interest or pleasure in activities they used to enjoy.
- Bad temper, irritability.
- General lethargy, fatigue and loss of energy nearly every day.
- Fearful, tense, anxious, withdrawn.
- A drop in performance at school.
- Disruptive/destructive behaviour.
- Mood swings.
- Imagined illnesses where there is no medical cause.
- Appetite variations.
- Changes in sleeping habits.
- Bedwetting.
- Nightmares.

Reactions at different ages

The symptoms referred to above straddle the age groups and much depends upon the social environment and background from which the children come. If the parents are dysfunctional themselves, then the likelihood is that the children will be too.

If parents separate when children are babies or infants, the children will not remember a time when their father lived with them so they do not suffer the effects of the separation itself. There will not have been a change in their routine or life so far as they are aware and thus the impact of the separation is not felt by these children in the same way as it is felt by the father. In these situations it is the father's ongoing role that becomes significant and more crucial. We touched on this in Chapter 1 and we look at this in depth in Chapter 4.

Small children between the age of about 5 and 10 are more likely to say they do not feel well or that they do not want to go to school. Their way of expressing they are not happy is by their actions rather than their words. They may become more aggressive and uncooperative or withdraw into themselves. For young children in particular there is a need for consistency in their lives and they are most seriously affected where it is lacking. The loss of daily contact with their father rocks their foundations. The security point again! Little children may not fully understand that their parents have stopped loving each other and, even if they do grasp that point, they may think that their parents will stop loving them too. Or, as we saw above, they may think that their father is leaving because he does not love them any more. They may become mistrustful.

Children between the age of 11 and 16 are very aware of discord, situations and atmospheres. They can feel guilty about parental conflict especially if they believe they are the source of the conflict between their parents. Older children may feel deep sadness and loss. Their schoolwork may suffer and behavioural problems are common. As teenagers they may experiment with drugs and/or alcohol and generally go off the rails. Teenagers may have trouble with their own relationships and experience problems with self-esteem that will follow them into their adult life.

How the parents' relationship impacts on the children's reaction

The effects of the relationship breakdown on the children are determined during the relationship and depend on the level of conflict between the parents. After a split, parenting and raising children may be more difficult. If there were conflicts or disagreements over parenting before the split, those problems will usually be worse and not better afterwards. Interestingly enough, the termination of a destructive relationship will probably be beneficial to the children because it removes them from an antagonistic and stressful environment. For these children this will be a welcome release from an adversarial and dysfunctional home life, and better for their psychological well-being.

What a father can do to help

We have looked at ways to resolve issues amicably in Chapter 2 and we will look at the post-separation relationship in Chapter 4. As indicated above, the parents' relationship has a direct bearing upon how they handle and react to the needs of their children. How skilfully parents can handle or mishandle their interactions with each other, and the children, makes a difference. Recognizing that children have a right to expect to continue to have the love and support of, and to enjoy a happy relationship with, both parents is very positive.

Put them first

A father can really help his children by letting them know that, whatever happens, he will always be fully committed to them and will love them, listen to them, and take account of their views. Because children tend to feel insecure at this time it is crucial to keep commitments and promises made to them. If a father cannot do that he must explain to them why not, otherwise they are left feeling that he does not really care even though that is not the case at all. What an adult may not consider to be a big issue may be a major issue for a child. Children's reactions will be influenced by a father's ability to provide continuing emotional support and this sense of security. The children will fare best knowing that both parents remain involved with them, even though the family no longer lives together.

Be alert to signs of distress

It is necessary to be alert to any signs of distress that they portray and to look out for warning signals. By carefully observing his children, a father will see if they have anxieties and concerns and can give them the attention they need. If there is cause for concern it helps if a father can talk to the mother or at least agree that help from a qualified health professional – generally the GP in the first instance – could be beneficial.

Things a father should not do

Most of these points apply to both parents, not just fathers.

- After the parties have separated, and while they sort out all the arrangements, they should try to avoid the children being caught in the crossfire.
- Long legal wrangles or pressure for the children to 'choose sides' can be particularly harmful to them and can add to their distress. Children should not be faced with having to choose which parent is the better parent.
- Do not talk about the children within their earshot.
- Do not argue in front of the children.
- Do not manipulate, pressure or lie in order to make the children take sides.
- Do not use the children as messengers or spies.
- Do not exclude the children's involvement with the other members of the family, for example grandparents.
- Do not withhold information from the other parent.
- Do not speak negatively about the other parent. When children hear negative

remarks about one of their parents they internalize it. This holds true for remarks concerning stepparents, grandparents and extended family members and any other significant person in the children's lives.

- This is not a time to use the children as a sounding board or an emotional prop.
- Do not make it difficult for the children to express their feelings. They need to vent them. Do not tell them how they should feel.

The children's wishes

A child's perspective

Children have a different perspective from adults. It should never be assumed that because the children do not talk about their concerns that they do not have any. However, they do like to be consulted and for their views to be heard. What are their views? Have these been taken on board? It is important to listen to what they have to say.

What are the children thinking?

A father needs to take into account what the children really want when making arrangements and talk to them, but remember that children often feel torn as they have divided loyalties and because they do not want to hurt their mother, or for their father to be cross with them, may sit on the fence. The children may have concerns and expectations for example regarding a father's new partner. Children may feel resentful of a new partner if they see that partner as the reason why their father moved out. They may think that he loves his new partner more than them.

Needs and requirements in light of age and understanding

It is necessary to look at what the children's needs are and consider what the difficulties are for them. It is very stressful for a child to see one or either or both his/her parents emotionally stressed. Children, even very small ones, are sensitive to atmospheres and pick up on when something is wrong. This in turn impacts on them and they are affected.

Where mature children are involved it is important to listen to their views. Their views may have an important influence on the terms of what is being discussed between the parents and the end result.

In any settlement where there are dependent children, their needs and welfare will need to be reflected in the terms of any agreement and, of course, in contested proceedings the child's welfare is the first consideration of the court and will be treated as paramount.

We look at the circumtances where a child may be made a party to court proceedings, his/her separate representation and proposals for reform in Chapter 11.

Stepchildren

The significance for them of the breakdown of the second relationship

In Chapter 1 we looked at how the family unit is changing. In Chapter 4 we look at remarriage and the introduction of a child to a new partner and potential stepparent. But what about the scenario whereby children have already been through the natural parents marriage breakdown, and one or both of the parents remarry and then one or both those second relationships fail? This situation is, unfortunately, quite common because over half divorced parents marry again and sadly second marriages are more likely to fail than first ones, and therefore there will be many stepchildren affected by these breakdowns.

The breakdown of the first relationship is going to be bad enough for the children, but if there is a second split the children will go through trauma again, especially if they have become attached to the stepparent. In this situation a child's loyalties may have been torn between the natural parents and now they may be torn even further.

All the factors we have looked at above apply here as well.

Chapter 4
Post-separation fatherhood

The post split father/child relationship

What is going to happen?

What happens to the father/child relationship after the parents' relationship breaks down? How does he maintain a meaningful relationship with his children? We have already talked about the importance of a father and his role. We touched on maintaining that role in Chapter 1. Many fathers say that, post split, their fathering role is never quite the same, but that they do manage to carve out a satisfactory role for themselves. For those who do achieve continuity in the fathering role there are, at the very least, transitional problems and glitches along the way. Very few indeed can achieve a completely smooth transition. Others report that they are unable to maintain a role at all.

Carving out a new role?

In the next chapter we look at how and why the father's relationship with the mother is so important for maintaining quality contact with the children. Sustaining an active and supporting role in the children's lives is weighted against a father if the inter-parental relationship is poor, and this is the case no matter how much a father loves his children and wants to spend time with them. This is seen by a father as the biggest obstacle to contact and has serious implications for his relationship with his children. Fathers often have to jump through hoops in their attempts to fulfill a meaningful role.

Where inter-parental relationships work well, the father/child relationship generally does too. This does not mean that if the parents have problems then the father and his children will, just that it will be harder for a father to be involved and build the relationship he would like to have with his children. He will have to make a conscious effort to be a part of their lives and for fathers who do want to be a regular part of their children's lives it can be very tough.

Fathers feel that after the parties split there is always the danger that their relationship with their children will slide. Sometimes the battle against the mother for contact is too much and fathers give up fighting for it, or put up with severely reduced contact. To an outsider looking in, it may appear that the father has just walked away from his children because he simply does not care about them, and wants to shirk his responsibilities. Dubbed by the media as 'dead beat dads'.

Appearances can, of course, be deceptive. Fathers also state that one cause of major problems is the mother's new partner and the stepfather of their children. We look at this below.

Choices for fathers

Giving up

Into this category fall those fathers who have had to make extraneous efforts to maintain contact in a hostile climate. They may have had to deal with severely frustrated contact and/or court proceedings, but have still been unable to obtain any decent level of contact with their children. The emotional, physical and financial costs of continuing to pursue contact have taken their toll and they see their decision to abandon the fight as in the best interests of everyone, particularly their children. They argue that they are not opting out but making a sacrifice. These fathers do not wish for their children to be embroiled in bitter court proceedings and caught in the middle between their parents wrangling over them. Many of these fathers remain bitter and harbour resentment against the mother whom they regard as vindictive and manipulative, and disillusioned with a legal system which they believe does not address the problems of being a non-resident parent.

Hanging in there

These fathers may have to face exactly the same problems as in the category above; they cannot communicate with the mother and face the same hostility. They are determined to keep the father/child relationship going by surmounting obstacles made by the mother so as to maintain a degree of contact with their children, if nothing else. They feel deeply unhappy with their situation, the continuing struggle, the enduring bitterness and conflict, and at times feel like giving up too. These fathers continue to maintain a presence, even if only a shadowy one, and take every opportunity to press for more contact if and when the occasion does arise.

Reinventing a role for father

Fathers say that the reality is that, being removed from the children for the bulk of the time, impacts upon their role as fathers. Understandably a 'two-day a fortnight father' feels he is losing out on the day to day routine of the children. Of course, this is a direct consequence of a father leaving the family home – which generally happens even if he did not initiate the separation – and for those fathers who did not want to separate in the first place this may be more of a tragedy. It is very difficult to recreate the same role in an abnormal situation where fathers are, in effect, stepping in and out of the children's lives. This is why children are often spoilt on contact visits, as the father tries to compensate for not being there all the time. Of course, this can backfire because the mother often says that the father disturbs the children's normal routine and equilibrium and therefore objects to contact. So this becomes a Catch 22 situation for the father.

Making the most of contact: pointers for fathers

Faced with the reality of limited contact, compared with the relationship that the father used to be able to enjoy with his children, is it any surprise he is tempted to spoil them when they are with him on contact visits or holidays?

Make contact as normal as possible

Clearly fathers want to treat their children, but it is when it turns into a competition between mother and father as to whose company the children enjoy most that difficulties arise. A complaint mothers make is that fathers deliberately go out of their way to undermine them. They do this by giving the children a better time than mothers are able to provide on a day to day basis. This causes resentment, although in the circumstances it is only to be expected that fathers may want to indulge their children when they do see them.

Keeping the children entertained

Fathers sometimes worry about what they should do to entertain the children on contact visits. They worry that the children will be bored. When the parties were together they had a routine and probably the children were happy with that. Fathers might be surprised to find that their children are often just happy spending time with them. The problem stems from the fact that fathers want to make contact special because of the limited time they have to spend with their children.

Disciplining the children

On contact visits, fathers generally tend to be more lenient. Fathers do not want to spend the time with their children disciplining them. One father told me that his little boy was very badly behaved on his Saturday contact visit, but he did not want to discipline him because that would probably have meant ruining the day, and so he let it pass as the time he had with him was very precious.

Avoid making any negative comments about their mother

Children sometimes repeat things that their mother may have said about their father which may not be altogether pleasant. It is better for the father to ignore the comment, or to deal with it casually, rather than to make a big issue out of it or respond with some vicious barb because, whatever she has said, she is still their mother. This works both ways. If a father has negative feelings towards the mother he should avoid directing them toward the children.

Be prepared to give a little

No agreement should ever be so carved in stone that it cannot be varied if necessity dictates. This applies even if there is a court order setting out the arrangements. Unfortunately, many parents rigidly adhere to these agreements, fearful that the slightest element of flexibility will weaken their position. It is a question of being flexible in response to a reasonable request.

Do not pressurize the children

Children need time to adjust to a change in their circumstances, different routines and unfamiliar surroundings. They now have two homes and in the initial stages moving between both parents' homes is emotionally trying. Parents need to think about how all this is affecting them. Children need to be surrounded by items with which they are familiar. They are more comfortable and relaxed knowing that they have their own possessions in both homes and that they will be there when they return.

Dealing with problems

Reasons for resisting contact

There are many reasons why children may resist contact. The most common reasons, with which many fathers are already familiar and that they may have to face, are as follows:

- They may not like his new partner or related family members. If the new partner already has children there may be stepsibling rivalry.
- The children reach an age when they have other commitments. They may want to go out with friends, they may have to study for exams, have extra-curricular school activities, and other interests that have become very important to them. Because they cannot spend so much time with their father this does not mean they no longer love him. It does not necessarily mean that they do not want to see him or that their mother is preventing them from seeing him. Fathers have to review contact arrangements and to reconsider their own role as the children grow older.

What to do if the children won't see their father

A father cannot force his children into wanting to spend time with him. This just makes matters worse. For example, if they do not like his new partner or they feel that he walked out on them, then the father has to take a step back and accept the situation. They may lash out at their father because they are hurting and he must not lash back. In time they may be able to rebuild their relationship with him. A father can often re-negotiate the relationship with his child but only when the child is ready. Sometimes he just has to be patient as with time they may accept the changes in his life; as they grow older they will have a better understanding of the situation. However, this is easier said than done.

Fathers feel rejected and insecure when their children do not want to see them. They believe that their children do not love them any more and this hurts. They fear that they are losing their children. It does not help if a mother does not want to encourage the father's relationship. It may give her the excuse she has been looking for to reduce the contact. It is very difficult for a father to know what is best to do. All he can do is to make it clear he loves his children unconditionally and that he is there if they need him.

Problems may ease in relation to the children once financial matters are resolved in a good many cases, but mothers do hold the trump card. You can tell a father that time will heal and when the children are a little older they can decide with their feet, but you try telling that to a father of a two-year-old child who is totally distraught that he cannot see his child. It might be a solution but it is hardly a satisfactory one.

External influences: dealing with new partners

Adjustments to be made

The break up may have been caused because one party has found a new partner. If not for that reason, they may have found someone since the split. They may decide to live together; they may subsequently marry. The new partner may have children of his/her own. Whatever the facts, a number of adjustments have to be made for both parents and the children. Sometimes the partner who has been left on their own can be very resentful of the other party's new-found relationship and happiness, and problems bubble under the surface which can then manifest themselves in contact problems. The children themselves may have issues.

Introducing the children to a new girlfriend

One of the problems for a father with a new partner is introducing the children to her. When does he do this? What will they think? How will they react? He needs to be aware of his children's feelings. Loving parents will be concerned with any effect on the children. If the parties are arguing over contact and an application to the court has been made, the court will want to know whether the father is offering a stable environment since the court will not want the children exposed to different partners over a short period. Is the relationship stable? A father does not want to introduce his children to his new girlfriend, for them to become attached to her and then for her to suddenly disappear. This breeds insecurity.

Older children may be critical (or even jealous) of their father's new girlfriend. This is another example of where they may think that he does not love them any more, or as much, or be able to spend time with them. These are issues that will have to be dealt with.

Their mother may oppose the father introducing the children to his new girlfriend on the grounds that it is too soon, too disruptive and, even if initial contact takes place, she may firmly object to overnight contact taking place until the children have adjusted. She simply may not like his new partner. We look at reasons for a mother's opposition to contact in Chapter 5. This can cause a problem if prior to the father forming a new relationship he had overnight contact with the children. If the children react well to a new partner it makes it easier. If they do not like her, then there are problems.

The mother's new partner and its relevance to the father/children relationship

There is often resentment on the part of a father when the mother finds a new partner, they start living together and/or she remarries. A father's fear is not just that the new man might supplant him in the children's affections. The resentment often flows from the fact that the stepfather can see his stepchildren anytime he wants but the natural father can see his children only as agreed or by order of the court. That is a dire situation for a father to be in. It is intolerable.

Of course, a father can be deliberately awkward and if he wants to sabotage the mother's new relationship may use the children as pawns and oppose everything the mother wants to do, for example in relation to the children's schooling or medical treatment.

In one particular case the father was a bully and there had been physical violence to the mother during the marriage, which was why she divorced him. They had one child, a little boy. She remarried and had another child and her son developed a very good relationship with his stepfather. The natural father then began a major 'contact campaign'. He said that the mother was denying him contact, and not consulting him on issues relating to his son. The mother had not denied the father contact but the father took issue with the mother over everything relating to their son. She found it difficult to deal with him and if he did not agree with something he would threaten a court application, and then go and make it. This mother lived under the continual threat of the father making an application as soon as a contentious point arose between them. Instead of trying to resolve matters with her amicably, his solution was to make an immediate application to the court. On several occasions the first indication the mother had that there was a problem, was when she was notified of a forthcoming hearing in the post.

And another thing…

When parents remarry the mother/child bonds tend to be strengthened while the father/child ties are strained. Apparently, second wives are less likely to want to raise someone else's children, although there are many cases where both parties have children from previous marriages and it does not pose a problem at all.

Mother moving away

Generally, the further the distance between the children and the father, the harder it is for him to maintain contact with them and less likely that he can visit regularly. That is bad enough. Should a mother want to move to the other side of the world the situation becomes critical. For a father who has a regular pattern of contact with his children and/or has already had to surmount innumerable obstacles to ensure that he has a degree of contact, this is a nightmare situation. Even where the mother is committed to contact with the father taking place, the reality is that no matter what her best intentions are, if she is on the other side of the world, at best that contact will be severely limited.

The welfare of the child is paramount, so is it in the children's best interest to see their father maybe a couple of times a year? How will the child be able to build a strong relationship with both parents? The move abroad prevents this from happening. Inevitably a father's contact would be severely reduced to holiday contact and he would therefore be denied involvement in the general upbringing of his child. Unless the father happens to be a millionaire, and most are not, he may not be able to afford to visit his children frequently.

If a mother wishes to relocate out of the UK with the children and the father does not agree she must make an application to the Court for leave to remove them. We will look at this in Chapter 13.

Contact with the extended family

Grandparents

Contact subject to parental control
In the majority of cases when parties are together, the degree of contact that the children have with their grandparents will depend upon the parents because they control the contact. Should the parents not have a close relationship with the grandparents they will probably not promote the grandchild/grandparent relationship.

Post separation contact
After separation, the amount of contact children have with the grandparents is governed by the parent with whom the children live. Since this is invariably the mother, generally the maternal grandparents retain a closer link because they form part of her extended family to whom she will turn for support. Unless the mother has a good relationship with the paternal grandparents their relationship with the grandchildren will suffer. Grandparents can help the children because if they have supporting roles they can reduce the disruption of the parent's separation. Grandparents provide the bulk of non-parental childcare in this country; it is estimated that this is at least 60%.

In one case the parties separated when their son was sixteen months old. The father remarried and moved far away. The mother had no alternative but to return to work full-time in order to make ends meet, so she entrusted the daily care of her son to her own parents since she could not afford child care. The maternal grandparents played a pivotal role in this child's upbringing. They cared for him every week day from 8am to 6pm until he went to school, and thereafter all the school holidays until he reached the age of fourteen.

Is promotion of contact generally dependent upon the mother or not?
A great deal depends upon the mother's relationship with the father's parents. Some mothers have amicable ongoing relationships with their in-laws and freely facilitate contact. In the case referred to above, the mother encouraged contact with the paternal grandparents, and she herself had an excellent relationship with the paternal grandmother. Unfortunately, not all cases are like this and in many cases the paternal grandparents will be limited to contact when the father has contact visits – and even that could be severely curtailed if the mother raises objections.

Additionally, if it was the mother who had previously encouraged contact with the father's parents and no longer does so, then the split will be detrimental to the paternal grandparent/grandchild relationship. Thus the loss/lack of contact with paternal grandparents might occur not because the mother prevents it, but because the father leaves the responsibility for maintaining contact with her, even though they are now apart.

There has been considerable debate about the importance of maintaining contact between grandchildren and their grandparents and the positive contribution which grandparents make to their grandchildren's lives. Grandparents are often key confidants for children facing enforced change since they represent stability and many children report having very close relationships with their grandparents.

Other family members

Children can feel torn when there are a number of other relatives pressing for contact. Usually children will have more contact with the relatives of the parent with whom they live. Contact may become more fragmented when parents remarry and step relations are introduced.

Parents see their relatives as important sources of support and turn to them in times of crisis. They may also be dependent on their family for emotional and financial support and this can be ongoing and sometimes that puts a strain on those relationships too. Given the heavy reliance on the extended family during this period, it is difficult to imagine how a father who does not have an extended family copes alone at this time.

We examine how the law treats grandparents and members of the extended family in Part II.

Chapter 5
Friend or foe: dealing with your ex

Working together

Acting in the children's best interests...

Parents must try to avoid settling old scores by using their children as pawns. They need to cooperate and support each other for the sake of the children, keep the lines of communication open and put their children first. Even though they no longer live together in the same household, fathers will always be fathers and they and their children need quality and quantity time together. They are ex-husbands and ex-partners but not ex-fathers!

Facilitating contact

A mother needs to facilitate contact and encourage the children's relationships with their father. There will always be exceptions. For example, where a father has abused, neglected or deserted a child, or where there has been domestic violence and the mother opposes contact, what is in the best interests of the child will be something the court will have to decide. We look at a mother's justification for preventing contact further below. How the court deals with these issues is addressed in Part II.

In cases where both parties are genuinely acting in their children's best interests, and the problems in the above paragraph do not apply, they may find some way to sort out the contact arrangements. In previous chapters we have talked about avoiding conflict and agreeing arrangements but we have not looked at the arrangements themselves.

Contact schedules

Parties may work out a contact schedule and agree dates for contact, where that contact will take place, how long the contact visits will be, including collection and return times. They should consider the arrangements for staying contact and holiday contact. Will the children stay overnight? What are the holiday plans? What is feasible? If the children have a routine, that will need to be factored into the arrangements. Do the children have extra-curricular activities? Can contact arrangements be made to fit around them?

Both parties have to expect that very occasionally arrangements need to be altered. Although last minute changes should be avoided, sometimes this cannot be helped due to some unforeseen event. For fathers who travel abroad on business, agreeing a rigid contact schedule in advance can be very difficult because it is not always possible to schedule business arrangements and trips around contact. Sometimes business plans are changed at the last minute and are not within the father's control. Flexibility is required on the part of both parties if contact arrangements are to work well.

The parental relationship

Although the parties' relationship has come to an end, their parental relationship is ongoing. They need to work on that relationship together as parents for the sake of the children. Conflict between parents makes contact very difficult. Probably the most accurate test as to whether the parties have adjusted after their split is to look at the level of conflict between them. It is not a good sign if parents are constantly at each other's throats and it is certainly not healthy for children to be caught in the crossfire.

The goal of everybody, advisors included, should be to reduce conflict between former partners thereby reducing the negative impact on the children.

Parental Interaction

A father's relationship with the mother is highly significant when it comes to his ongoing relationship with his children. Fathers confirm that the 'type' of relationship they have with the mother has a direct bearing upon the quality of contact they enjoy with their children, and that the majority of disputes arise from ongoing or recurring conflict.

Relationships between former partners fall into a number of categories. They may have a relatively positive relationship and can separate out their issues, enabling each parent to have a quality relationship with the children. They may be amicable or able to tolerate each other for the benefit of the children. In this way the 'emotional' disruption of the break up is reduced. On the other hand, they may have a very negative relationship where conflict has a nasty habit of breaking out at the slightest sign of tension between the parties, and where there is a lack of support, cooperation and trust. This causes 'emotional' stress for everybody involved.

What type of relationship do the parties have?

Friends

Parties may fall into this category because for one reason or another they have decided to separate, but the decision is mutual and often based on the best interests of the children. They may have just drifted apart and although they may not 'love' each other any more, still like and respect one another and recognize that each parent has a valid contribution to make to the children so they work together.

If one party does have any negative feelings towards the other, he/she does not let those feelings interfere with the parental relationship. Because they put the children's welfare above their own they have workable and flexible child arrangements and emotional disruption to the children is minimized. This type of relationship is not very commonplace and more parties fall into the next category.

Formal acquaintances

If parties fall into this category then they will probably be less at ease with each other and child arrangements will therefore be on a more formal footing. There may be conflict between them in relation to their own issues, but they manage it and do not allow this to spill over into their relationship with the children. So, although they will not be friends, they will make compromises for the sake of the children and make agreements in their best interests which still have the necessary flexibility to work well. Both parties will make joint decisions over important matters relating to the children and exercise their parental responsibilities well. This relationship allows the children to maintain a healthy relationship with both parents.

Warring parties

If parties fall into this category then there will be a lot of anger, bitterness and resentment in their own relationship which has not been dealt with which spills over into the parental relationship. They will find it very difficult to separate out and discuss child issues and argue over the smallest points always re-opening old wounds when they try to negotiate.

Their relationship is strained and, even if they can come to some form of agreement regarding the children, there is little flexibility in the arrangements. This means that contact will be difficult and the children will be caught up in the midst of it all and have torn loyalties. Members of each party's respective families may become involved in the squabbles and the children will be affected by the poor relationship.

Sworn enemies

If parties fall into this category their own relationship problems dominate and they cannot communicate on child issues. They see each other as enemies and dwell on all the negative aspects of their relationship and lose focus. There is a great deal of anger for one reason or another and as it is not dealt with matters do not improve. Since the parties cannot agree child arrangements, they invariably resort to court proceedings to battle it out, and this in turn causes more conflict. The contact is constantly frustrated and they enter a vicious circle of conflict.

Everybody is affected and children become pawns. Every opportunity is used to score points against each other. A father in these situations often fights harder for contact in the initial stages, but over a period of time may gradually withdraw to reduce and/or avoid conflict because he cannot continue with a full scale war for various reasons. In such circumstances the father and children both suffer.

Disconnected partnerships

Into this category fall those relationships where, after the parties split, the father moves away completely and all contact is discontinued. The father generally withdraws from his former partner's life.

Parents may start off in one category and move into another. Many couples start off in the warring parties' category and then move into the formal acquaintances' category. This may be due to time healing matters between them or because they have made the conscious effort to improve their relationship for the sake of the children. Open communication between parents is the key. It is important for each parent to continue to communicate with the other no matter how they feel.

Communicate to negotiate

It takes two...

It cannot be emphasized enough that in order to resolve matters both parties need to communicate. Each party will have views and want those views heard, but the way those views are communicated to the other party can make a difference. So how can they communicate constructively and productively?

Communicating effectively

The common ground between the parties should be to find a solution that is in the best interests of their children. If they keep that goal in sight, then they will both attempt to communicate. Neither party can force the other to communicate nor to make an agreement, but for a father there are things he should bear in mind if he plans to try and resolve child issues with the mother. He needs to:

- Be clear about the issues he wants to discuss and think about areas of potential conflict.
- Decide where he is going to meet the mother. Think about a neutral location.
- Start off with issues that are not in dispute.
- Think about the children's wishes. Has he talked to them and asked them what they want?
- Listen to what the mother has to say and explain why he holds a particular view on a certain issue.
- Be prepared that there are things he may need time to consider and not feel that he has to give an immediate response and also be prepared to compromise. Maybe neither party has considered all the options. Give and take is important in these situations.
- Decide what his boundaries are. How far is he prepared to negotiate? What is negotiable and what is not?
- Keep reminding himself that he is communicating to resolve matters amicably in his children's best interests not his.

Maternal gatekeeping

As we have seen, where the parents' own relationship is poor then problems with contact are compounded. In such circumstances fathers are faced with a dilemma. They want to see their children but are often thwarted. Fathers mention situations where the mother prevented contact with the children, and the health, safety or wishes of the children had nothing to do with the refusal!

Sabotaging the father/child relationship

When fathers leave the family home and there is conflict, one of their concerns is that they are going to be dependent upon the mother to facilitate contact and to promote the father-child relationship. Fathers refer to mothers actively trying to sabotage their relationship with their children and trying to 'poison' the children against them in order to destroy a previously loving relationship.

In the United States this is known as Parental Alienation Syndrome. This is where mothers attempt to programme the children and use psychological tactics to destroy the relationship, even though outwardly they may appear to support contact. There are a number of factors to consider including the strength of the father/child bond in the first place, the ages of the children, what the children might actually decide they want for themselves and external influences such as the mother's new partner.

What do fathers consider to be sabotage?

Sabotage does not just relate to the contact visits, but the whole father/child relationship. Mothers may try to exclude fathers from issues relating to the children and in effect sideline or in drastic cases oust them from their lives altogether. The following list is not exhaustive but it includes common complaints made by fathers against mothers:

- The mother calls the father at the last minute to change the contact arrangements or to cancel the visit by which time the father is probably on his way.
- The father arrives to pick up his children to be told that they are ill.
- The father arrives to pick up his children and there is nobody at home.
- The father calls to speak to his children and the mother either makes an excuse for him not to speak to them, says they are out, busy or refuses to allow him to speak to them.
- The children do not receive the cards and presents that the father sends through the post because the mother withholds them.
- The mother does not inform the father about medical, schooling and other important matters and constantly tries to make important decisions about the children without consulting the father. For example, when the father does not attend a parents' evening or school event, about which the mother has failed to inform him, she then tells everyone that he cannot be bothered and is not interested in the children.
- The mother encourages the children to regard her new partner as their father.
- The mother says that the father is irresponsible and that he does not care for

the children properly when they are with him.

- The mother blames the father if the children are badly behaved saying that it is his contact visits that disturb them.
- The mother says the father tries to undermine her relationship with the children on their contact visits.

Sabotage by mother or justifiable position?

Although from a father's perspective a mother may appear to be sabotaging contact, this may not be her intention at all. Some mothers may genuinely believe they are acting in the best interests of their children, even if it is an ill-founded belief and without any justification whatsoever. Fathers would argue that many mothers are being deliberately obstructive as a means of exacting revenge on them. Unfortunately, this is true in a number of cases, but there are situations where a mother has real cause for concern; matters are often neither black nor white but a variable shade of grey.

Examples of reasons for maternal sabotage provided by fathers

The following list is not exhaustive:

- The mother regards the father as a bad lot. He is not worthy to be the father of her children. Even though the parental relationship has failed this should not adversely impact on the father's relationship with his children. One father told me that he felt very guilty that he could not make his wife happy and he was totally responsible for the breakup of their marriage, but that she was now trying to punish him by being as awkward as possible when it came to contact.
- The parties may be caught up in an acrimonious financial battle, and a complaint sometimes made by fathers is that some mothers use contact as a tool to engineer a better financial settlement. By the same token, mothers sometimes claim that fathers put financial pressure on them as a means to force them to agree to more generous contact. Power struggles ensue...
- The mother may really hate the father. If he was the one to break up the relationship or walked out on the family she may use the children to exact her revenge on him. Alternatively, she may still want to be with the father and cannot accept that the relationship is over and uses the children to exert pressure.
- The mother has found a new life for herself and does not want the father to be part of it. She sees his intervention as bothersome and no longer desires to be in touch with him and wants to cut him off.
- The children may be all the mother has, she has become emotionally dependent on them, and is possessive of their love and jealous of their relationship with the father and fearful that in some way he might take them away from her.
- The mother feels resentful towards the father's 'generosity' to the children on contact visits, feeling she cannot compete.
- The father may have a new partner whom the mother resents and dislikes, and does not want as a rival for the children's affections, so finds reasons why the children cannot have contact with their father.

- The mother may have a new partner and she wants to establish her new family unit and for the children to think of him as their father.

A mother's justifiable concerns
Some examples:

- When the parties initially separate everybody involved is disrupted, especially the children. There are many adjustments that need to be made. A mother may argue at this time that if the children have weekend staying contact with their father this will cause disruption and that it will take her several days to re-establish their routine, therefore overnight contact is out of the question. Fathers complain about this, but the fact is this is often true. The problem for fathers is where this is an ongoing issue, even after a period of time, when both parties have settled into their new routines and homes.
- The father may have remarried or have a new partner and there are problems over introducing the children to that new partner and when staying contact may be appropriate. There are various factors to consider. The children may react well to the situation or they may not, and do not want to stay overnight anymore. Mothers report children being very distressed and bedwetting. Fathers see this as an excuse for avoiding contact.
- The mother may have genuine concerns about the welfare of the child. She may have reason to believe that the father is not looking after the children properly on contact visits. They may return from contact visits dirty, or with only half the clothes she sent them with, and they may not have been fed properly.
- In a situation where a father has set up home not with another woman but with another man and the mother is worried about the environment in which the child will be placed.
- Where there has been domestic violence.
- Where there has been abuse/maltreatment or the mother suspects it.
- Where the mother has other reasons to believe that the children are, or might be, in danger. Examples of this would be where the father was an alcoholic or drug addict or was mentally unstable.

A final word ...
Many mothers go to extreme lengths to ensure their children have flourishing relationships with their fathers and try to separate their own relationship from the parental one. These mothers actively support fathers' desires to stay involved with their families. By all accounts contact is an extremely sensitive and emotive issue and striking a balance is very difficult because each parent may have a different agenda and view of what is in the best interests of the children. Each case has its own specific set of circumstances, but one thing is certain: a child has two parents for a reason and should have every opportunity to build a loving relationship with both of them.

Chapter 6
In brief: the law and legal system

The law in outline

The Children Act 1989

This Act is the principal statute dealing with children. The Act was introduced to simplify the law relating to children and to consolidate and unify the court system. When the Act came into force in October 1991 most of the existing children legislation was repealed.

The Act is divided into two parts: the first part relates to private law and the second part to public law. Under the Act private law means the law between individuals, for example parents, and relates to their rights over, responsibilities towards and proceedings in respect of children. Public law means the law relating to the responsibilities and proceedings in respect of children where public bodies are concerned. This covers local authority care cases.

Private law orders

There are five main types of private law order that the court can make under the Children Act and which are of interest to fathers, as follows:

- Parental responsibility order. The Children Act introduced a new concept of parental responsibility. Essentially what parental responsibility means is having the responsibility for taking all the important decisions in a child's life on a day to day basis. We look at parental responsibility in detail in Chapter 8.

The four other orders are known collectively as s8 orders:

- A residence order: If a party has a residence order this means their child will live with them.
- A contact order: If a party has a contact order (usually the father) this requires the person who has residence (usually the mother) to allow the child to visit or stay with the father or for other forms of contact to take place such as telephone calls, letters etc. We look at the different forms of contact in Chapter 14.

- Prohibited steps order: A father would apply for this order to prevent the mother taking a particular step without the prior consent of the court. It is an order for forbidding actions.
- Specific issue order: A father would apply for this order where he has, or may have, a disagreement about a specific question in connection with any aspect of parental responsibility for his child and he needs the court to direct how it will be resolved. It is an order permitting actions to take place.

Public law orders
It is not within the ambit of this book to deal with public law save where local authority proceedings impact upon a father's contact with his child. We will look at this briefly in Chapter 10.

Underlying principles under the Children Act
When the court makes any order under the Children Act relating to the upbringing of a child it will consider:

- The child's welfare. This shall be the paramount consideration of the court. There are a number of factors the court will review and these are known as the 'welfare checklist'. See below and Chapter 10.
- Whether to make 'no order'. Where the court is considering whether or not to make one or more orders under the Act, it may decide not to make ân order or any orders unless it considers that making an order would be better for the child than making no order at all. The Act assumes that parties will endeavour to make their own agreements. In other words, it has to be in the best interests of the child to make an order. This is known as the non-intervention principle.
- There must be 'no delay'. The court will want to deal with matters as quickly as possible. For a child several months is a long time. Delay could be detrimental. This is why the the timing of cases has to be regulated. Delay has been a major criticism of the court system. We look at measures introduced to deal with this in Chapter 10.

How the court decides

The court will have regard to seven factors when considering the welfare of the child:

- The ascertainable wishes and feelings of the child concerned, considered in the light of the child's age and understanding.
- The child's physical, emotional and educational needs.
- The likely effect on the child of any change of circumstances.
- The age, sex, background and any characteristics of the child which the court considers relevant.
- Any harm which the child is suffering or which the child is at risk of suffering.
- How capable each of the parents, and any other person in relation to whom the court considers the question to be relevant, is of meeting the child's needs.
- The range of powers available to the court under this Act in the proceedings in question.

Each of these factors is referred to in detail in Chapter 10.

The courts and court protocol

The courts

Jurisdiction

In private law matters, proceedings can be commenced in any court that has jurisdiction to deal with the case. The courts have jurisdiction to make s8 orders in the following situations:

- Where there are divorce proceedings between the parents.
- The child is habitually resident in England & Wales, that is has lived there for a settled period of time.
- The child is present in England & Wales and is not habitually resident in any other part of the UK.

Which courts deal with children matters?

The courts that deal with children matters in the first instance are the:

- The Family Proceedings Court which is part of the Magistrates Court.
- County Court.
- High Court.

We look at the Appeal process in Chapter 16.

Which is the right court for my case?

The Family Proceedings Courts do not deal with divorce. These courts generally deal with less complex cases and the magistrates sit in groups of two or three. Most magistrates are trained volunteers rather than lawyers, although there are increasing numbers of District Judges who now sit in these courts. If there are divorce proceedings these will be filed in a County Court which deals with family cases and an application under the Children Act will be made there within those proceedings. An unmarried father would make what is known as a free-standing application under the Children Act and he might start proceedings in either the Family Proceedings Court or the County Court.

The judges in the County Court are known as District Judges and hear private law family work. They are experienced in family work and sit alone. The Principal Registry in London is a Divorce County Court. The High Court can hear all types of Children Act applications. It will generally deal with the more complex cases, which could either be started there, or those which are transferred up to it from the other courts. For example, the cases it currently deals with include those involving complicated medical evidence, international issues, abuse and where children are making their own applications. Cases can be transferred down as well. It depends on the circumstances. The Children Act introduced a unified court system to make transfers between courts easier.

Court layout and dress

Family proceedings are more informal than other legal proceedings and generally held in chambers, which means they are in private and not open to members of the public unlike criminal proceedings. In these circumstances neither the judges nor the advocates wear gowns or wigs. The layout of the court varies from court to court. Usually the seating arrangements are more relaxed and the court is often a large room with the judge sitting at the head of a table and the parties and their advisors on either side.

The Principal Registry is in High Holborn, London. It deals specifically with family cases. In these courts the District Judge sits on a raised platform, there is a witness box and there are several rows with seating for the parties and their advocates. The Family Division of the High Court is based in London at the High Courts of Justice in the Strand. These courts are similar to the courts at the Principal Registry but much larger and less modern than the former.

There are instances where family proceedings are held in open court, which means the press and members of the public are allowed into court. Of particular relevance to fathers are committal proceedings for contempt of court orders. For example, where a mother refuses to hand over a child for contact and is hostile and repeatedly in breach of court orders, there is provision to apply for her to be committed to prison. This is rare and is explored in more detail in Chapter 14.

We look at reform re the openness of family court proceedings in Chapter 12.

Relevant court personnel

- Counter clerks. These form part of the administrative personnel. They are not legally qualified and therefore do not give legal advice. They have various roles but specifically there are clerks who deal with the issuing of applications, lodging of court forms, payment of court fees and listing of cases.
- Court clerks, Associates and Ushers. When parties and their advisors arrive at court they need to inform court staff that they are present. The court needs to know who is in attendance and the names of the parties and their representatives. In the County Court the clerk will be allocated to a District Judge. Any papers that the judge needs to review before the hearing must be handed to his clerk. The clerk will be present in court, and generally sits below and just in front or to the side of the District Judge. The clerks have a number of duties: they pass papers to the District Judge when they are handed up from the parties or their advisors, swear parties in if they are to give evidence, liaise with the listing office over hearing dates and draw up court orders made by the District Judge further to the hearing. They are not legally qualified. In the High Court the usher wears a black gown and literally ushers parties in and out of court. The associate's role is essentially the same as the court clerk.

Court address
How should the judges be addressed?

- Magistrates are referred to as: Your Worship, Sir or Madam.
- Deputy/District Judges as: Sir/Madam.
- County Court Judges as: Your Honour.
- High Court/Court of Appeal Judges as: My Lord (M'Lord), My Lady (M'Lady).

How are solicitors and barristers addressed in court?

- The judge will refer to them as Mr... or Mrs... or Miss... as appropriate.

- Solicitors refer to fellow solicitors as: My friend, Mr ... Mrs...or Miss as appropriate.
- Barristers tend to refer to each other as: My (learned) friend, Counsel for X.

Current developments

Working towards a network of Family Court Centres
The Department of Constitutional Affairs is planning to create a network of new-style family court centres in London. The plans were set out in a consultation document *London Regional Proposals for a Network of Family Court Centres* published on 31 July 2006. The Department of Constitutional Affairs published a summary of responses at the end of December 2006. The idea is to link County and Family Proceedings Courts together to ensure that, at all stages of a family case involving children, judges with the appropriate level of expertise needed to deal with the complexity of the case are available. The plan is to extend these proposals across the country.

Court personnel proposals
The Department of Constitutional Affairs is developing policies to change the process by which magistrates are authorised to sit and preside in the Family Proceedings Courts. Proposals were set out in its consultation paper *Authorisations to sit in Family Proceedings Courts and Youth Courts* published in November 2005. There are also plans afoot to review the use of judicial resources at High Court level. Following the consultation paper *Focusing Judicial resources appropriately: The Right Judge for the Right Case* published on 15 September 2006, policies are now being developed by the department to implement its plans.

Creating one simple set of Family Procedure Rules
A consultation document *Family Procedure Rules – a new procedural code for family proceedings* was published by Her Majesty's Courts Service (which is part of the Department of Constitutional Affairs) in August 2006. The aim is to create one set of court rules for all family proceedings (which we do not have at present). There are four key objectives: modernisation of language, harmonisation with the Civil Procedure Rules, a single unified code of practice and alignment in all levels of court.

For the purposes of this book the particularly relevant proposals in the consultation paper are possible changes to:

- The Statement of Arrangements form. This is the form in which the party applying for a divorce or dissolution of a civil partnership sets out his/her proposed arrangements for the children post-split. We look at what this involves in Chapter 9.
- The management of children's proceedings by incorporating existing guidelines for both private law and public law cases into the new rules. One of the relevant documents to be incorporated is the Private Law Programme. We look at this in Chapter 10.
- The forms used for applications under the Children Act. The logic is that if the

rules are amended then some of the existing forms will need amending to reflect this. At the same time, the idea is to make the forms more user-friendly with simplified language and more guidance notes.

- The process of Appeals from Family Proceedings Courts. We look at this in Chapter 16.
- The terminology used.

The role of solicitors and barristers

Both solicitors and barristers may appear in court on behalf of their clients in child cases. Solicitors provide ongoing legal advice to the client and deal with the day to day running, management and preparation of a case. They are responsible for the preparation of court bundles which generally contain the following documents: all the court applications, orders made by the court, statements of the parties, the welfare report, experts' reports and relevant correspondence as applicable to the particular case. They attend court hearings, either presenting the case themselves or attending as instructing solicitor with the barrister they have retained to present the case. The decision by a solicitor to appear at court depends upon the complexity of the case and the issues involved.

Generally, and there always exceptions, solicitors deal with early direction appointments and less contested applications in the court process. They are more inclined to instruct a barrister as the case progresses because the barrister is a specialist advocate. Barristers will be instructed to advise on the issues and briefed to appear on behalf of the client at court and present the case. There are Juniors and Leaders. A party has a Conference with Counsel and a Consultation with Leading Counsel, known as QCs, that is Queen's Counsel.

In children's proceedings an atmosphere of negotiation and cooperation between professionals is encouraged. They are supposed to be non-adversarial. Unfortunately, the very nature of the legal system encourages the opposite.

The court process

The basic procedure in children's cases is the same. The court application and process is addressed in detail in Chapter 10. Here we deal briefly with general procedure at every hearing.

General procedure

The person who makes the application is known as the Applicant and the person against whom the application is made is known as the Respondent. At each hearing the Applicant's advocate introduces the other advocate and the parties to the court. The parties stand while the judge enters the court, nod and remain standing until the judge sits.

The length of the hearing will vary depending upon the issues involved and the stage of the case. The case will be allocated a time in the court list – but sometimes cases overrun and there can be a considerable waiting period, particularly in the High Court.

If a parent has legal representation and does not attend at court it will not prevent the hearing proceeding, unless it is necessary for that particular parent to give evidence or an order has been made for the parent's attendance by the court itself. There are occasions where it is possible to obtain an order without the other party being notified and present at court. These are known as ex parte orders and we look at these in Chapters 10 and 15.

The courts are extremely cautious where a party is not represented by a solicitor and fails to attend a hearing. A party representing themselves is known as a litigant in person. We look at litigants in person in detail in Chapter 12. The court will ask the other side to provide documentary evidence that this party has been properly served with the proceedings and is aware of the hearing date. This involves producing a statement of service and/or sworn statement from process servers to prove that the party has been properly notified of the court hearing. If the court feels that there has been proper service of the papers, or the Applicant can show that all reasonable steps have been to taken to try and serve the Respondent, then an order may be made. Sometimes hearings are adjourned to a later date to allow time for further attempts at service to be made or for any other valid reason such as the non-attendance of a party because of illness. The circumstances of the case and the nature of the hearing will have a direct bearing upon the decision made by the court.

Unless it is a final hearing, or an interim hearing where the parties are to give evidence and are to be cross-examined (in other words where there are witnesses) it will be a case of the Applicant's advocate opening the case and outlining it to the court. Then the Respondent's advocate has the opportunity to make a speech to the court. A judge may ask further questions and there may be some interaction between each party's advocate and the judge to assist the judge in making his/her decision. The judges will then make the order.

At a final hearing the Applicant's advocate opens the case and calls all the witnesses in support of the Applicant's case and questions them on their evidence – that is the witness statements they have filed at court setting out their case and which have been served on the other party. This is known as examination in chief. The Respondent's advocate has the opportunity to cross-examine those witnesses. If the Court & Family Reporter who prepared the welfare report is present, he/she may be questioned. Once the Applicant has presented the evidence it is the turn of the Respondent and all of the Respondent's witnesses to give evidence. The Applicant can then cross-examine those witnesses. The Respondent's barrister then makes his closing speech followed by the Applicant's barrister. The judge will then give judgment. Sometimes judgment is reserved while the judge considers the issues.

What is CAFCASS?

This is the Children and Family Court Advisory and Support Service. Prior to 1 April 2001 when CAFCASS became operational, the Family Court Welfare Service was responsible for the preparation of the much-dreaded welfare report.

Fathers in particular raised concerns that many Family Court Welfare Officers did not have a social work qualification and that they spent little or insufficient time with a child and his or her family to assess the situation adequately. This was seen as a major failing because the welfare report carries so much weight in court. CAFCASS is now responsible for the preparation of these reports. Part of CAFCASS's duty is to support children and families to ensure that their voices are heard and to assist the courts to make decisions that are in the best interests of the children affected by family proceedings. Like its predecessor CAFCASS has been criticised for not delivering these services effectively and for underperforming. CAFCASS has also been criticised for being inadequately funded, having insufficient staff without proper training and no provision for that training.

Many recommendations have been made to make it more effective and plans to overhaul CAFCASS were set out in the CAFCASS *Every day matters* consultation paper published at the end of 2005. One of the aims is to reduce delay by assigning a CAFCASS officer to every case referrred to it within two days. The target date for this is April 2007. Following on from that the urgency of cases should be assessed within six weeks. In this way more problematic cases such as those involving issues of abuse or domestic violence and cases where a parent is intractable about contact will be addressed more quickly – at least that is what is hoped. The idea is to reduce the number of reports that need to be made by resolving more cases at an earlier stage thereby freeing up time to deal with the difficult cases. The major stumbling block to the plan is that there is still no effective mechanism in place to do this. In any event, there are concerns over whether CAFCASS will have sufficient funding and resources to be able to achieve and sustain the proposed improved service to any significant degree.

Another issue is that CAFCASS has a poor reputation among fathers; they are very mistrustful of the service. Certainly the majority of fathers I have spoken to who have had dealings with CAFCASS have very little to say in favour of it and are particularly concerned about whether CAFCASS officers have either the capabilty or expertise to assess cases correctly.

Chapter 7
Your solicitor

How do I find a good family solicitor?

It is very important to find a solicitor who is a specialist family practitioner and therefore fully up to speed with family law. There are tales of clients who have been given poor legal advice by a solicitor who is not a family law specialist and who have lost out as a result. The choice of solicitor is important because the way a case is conducted can have a major bearing on the outcome. There are many firms that have strong family law departments with specialists who can draw on each other's strengths and have the expertise to deal with all aspects of family law.

Personal recommendation

Most family solicitors obtain new clients through the referral process; either through former clients or business associates such as other solicitors, bankers, accountants and financial advisors. Personal recommendation from friends who have divorced recently or had problems over family issues such as contact is very common. It is worth asking friends which firm of solicitors they instructed and in particular who dealt with their case, why they instructed that firm and the quality of service that was provided. So far as quality of service is concerned, this covers not only the advice given but also how they were treated generally.

Reputation

A father might decide to instruct a firm of solicitors because he has heard they have an excellent reputation for family law or he wishes to instruct a particular solicitor because he has heard about his/her personal reputation. It depends upon the approach he is looking for. A hard-hitting lawyer specializing in family finance may not be suitable for children proceedings. It is all a question of balance. At the end of the day, he needs to have confidence in his solicitor and the solicitor needs to instill confidence into him.

Law Society

The Law Society is the regulatory body for solicitors. They will be able to assist a father in finding a family specialist in his area. If he wants to find out more information about a solicitor, that is, whether they are a Partner and how many years they have been qualified, the Law Society will be able to provide this information.

Resolution (formerly the Solicitors Family Law Association 'SFLA')

Resolution members are solicitors who are all family law specialists. Resolution has a Code of Practice for its members to adhere to. A copy may be obtained by contacting Resolution. Solicitors who are members of Resolution should endeavour to advise, negotiate and deal with issues constructively and quickly with a view to encouraging a settlement and try to avoid conflict. In children's cases the approach is to be conciliatory and the aim is to deal with the issues in a non-confrontational manner.

Where children are involved Resolution's code directs family solicitors to see their work as most important and to act accordingly.

Memberships

The Solicitor may be an Accredited Specialist on the Law Society Family Panel or Children Panel or Resolution accredited Family law specialist. A solicitor may also be a lawyer/mediator as we saw in Chapter 2. Additionally he/she may be a collaborative lawyer.

Collaborative lawyers

Collaborative law is a US-inspired process. It is based on the principle that parties are much more likely to reach a settlement if both they and their respective lawyers work together and agree from the outset of the case to try and settle the case out of court – with the proviso that if they cannot settle the case and it has to proceed to court, then neither of the lawyers involved in the collaborative process will represent the parties further.

The parties meet together with their lawyers (who must be specially trained as collaborative lawyers) to discuss financial and children arrangements, which means they keep control of the process while supported by their legal advisors. Although each party's lawyer is available to give advice during the meetings the emphasis is always on the parties themselves working together to reach a settlement. In order to provide the optimum chance for the parties to settle the case the lawyers can enlist support from other experts including mediators, counsellors, accountants and financial advisers.

Unfortunately, collaborative law is still in its early stages in this country and at present there are insufficient trained lawyers to offer a countrywide service nor is there public funding for it. The Collaborative Family Law Group was established in October 2003 and is now affiliated to Resolution. More solicitors are training in collaborative law as it increases in popularity. Bearing in mind the adversarial nature of our current legal process, collaborative law can only be a positive step forward.

Other considerations which may affect the choice of solicitor

How much they cost

Solicitors charge on an hourly basis, and their hourly rate will depend upon how senior they are and where they are based. It is important to find out how much that hourly rate is before the first meeting. Where funds are limited a party may be entitled to a contribution towards their costs. This used to be called Legal Aid. The Legal Services Commission (LSC) has now replaced the Legal Aid Board. Not all firms undertake LSC funded services so that is something to clarify initially.

Solicitors charge for all time spent on a file. This is called chargeable time. This includes telephone calls made to the solicitor by a client and calls they make to the client or to third parties in relation to the case. All correspondence received and sent out is charged for, including e-mails and faxes. A client will be charged for meetings, perusal of documents, analysis of documents, preparation of documents, conferences with the barrister, attendance at court, travel time to and from court and conferences, and the travel costs.

Case management

If there are a number of solicitors in a firm who specialize in family law it is important to find out if there will be anyone else working on the file and what their charge out rate is. It may well be that the Partner instructed may delegate the case to a more junior member of staff, such as an Assistant, to deal with on a day to day basis. The Partner will continue to oversee the file and the Assistant will keep the Partner informed and refer to the Partner on important matters. From the client's point of view this has two implications:

- There is another point of contact and this is very useful if the Partner is often unavailable, in court, on holiday or ill, and
- This should reduce the costs.

Sometimes clients are not very happy about a more junior member of staff dealing with their case because the whole reason why they may have instructed a firm in the first place is that they want a particular solicitor to act for them. The reality is that Partners with busy practices will have to delegate work to a junior member of staff because they cannot handle all the work themselves and it is not cost effective for them to do so. However, Partners who manage their practices well will not delegate work to a more junior member of staff who is incapable of dealing with it. They will inform the client, and explain why they are delegating the matter and that they will oversee the file. They should also introduce their Assistant to the client at the earliest opportunity.

If clients have any concerns about the quality of work or the advice they are receiving they should feel able to raise them. Clients should never feel that they cannot question the progress of their case. The client is paying for the advice received and if there are queries about who is dealing with the work, or any of the work being undertaken, it should be questioned sooner rather than later in order that any problems can be addressed and rectified.

Personal qualities to look out for

Family solicitors have different styles. Feeling confident and comfortable with the solicitor instructed is crucial.

Affability

Obviously the solicitor/client relationship is a professional one, but the very nature of the work makes it much more 'personal' as family clients have to provide solicitors with intimate details of their lives. Therefore it is very important for a family client to be able to relate well to his/her solicitor and to build up a rapport with him/her. A client wants and needs a solicitor who is approachable, not gruff and standoffish. Clients like to feel that they can trust their solicitors implicitly and that they are patient, sympathetic and empathetic but also constructive, objective and polite, and firm when needs be.

Availability

The nature of family work is such that the solicitor will have a very hectic schedule and cannot always be there at the very instant a client calls. He/she may be on the 'phone or in a meeting or at court. If a client leaves repeated messages and calls are not returned then he needs to find out if the messages have been passed on or where his solicitor is and why he has not received a response. A solicitor's secretary can be of invaluable assistance to a client. It is important to build up a good rapport with the secretary because at the very least she will be able take an accurate message in her boss's absence and she may be able to deal with the query. Obviously she cannot give legal advice, but she will be familiar with the file so is a very good point of contact.

Ability

Clients also need someone who is in command of the subject and can advise thoroughly on their case, who has a grasp of all the issues and who can instill confidence and, of course, who acts constructively.

Characteristics to avoid

Arrogance

Solicitors who denigrate other solicitors to boost themselves are unprofessional because they inflame the situation between the parties. In family cases this is particularly detrimental and can do a great deal of damage. Confrontational solicitors will turn the process into a battle because they like to win. The whole case is in danger of turning into a battle of egos between the parties and their solicitors because this unconstructive behaviour promotes conflict.

Aggression

Sometimes family lawyers have to be very tough to fight their client's corner, but a party cannot negotiate if his/her solicitor turns every issue into a battle. Being tactical is a completely different point. Negotiation requires skill and is time consuming but is likely to be far more productive than aggressive correspondence.

Antagonism

A father should watch out for actions backfiring. He has to live with the consequences of any legal action taken long after his solicitor closes the file. If the solicitor makes his job more difficult then he should consider instructing a different solicitor.

The solicitor/client relationship

Giving and receiving advice

Instructing the solicitor

It is for the client to instruct the solicitor and for the solicitor to advise the client. The client should listen to the advice, but if he is dissatisfied with all or part of it and feels unhappy about pursuing a course of action proposed then he should make his instructions understood and not be forced into taking any action with which he is uncomfortable. If he has doubts about the advice he should take a second opinion.

Seeking clarification

If anything is unclear the solicitor should be asked to explain, otherwise the client may find himself going down a path he never intended. The solicitor will advise on the facts provided by the client, so a client needs to tell the solicitor everything to enable him/her to advise properly. Sometimes a solicitor will only be able to give initial advice, if full details of the case have not been provided.

Help to keep the costs down

In order to keep costs down, the client should try to be as organized as possible and be clear about what he wants to discuss with the solicitor before making the call or attending the meeting. By producing any information/documents requested as quickly as he can and by dealing with any queries his solicitor raises promptly, he should be able to cut down his costs.

Terms of business and costs

The costs letter

The Law Society requires all solicitors to inform clients in writing about their terms of business. The terms of business letter or letter of engagement will set out details of the solicitors who will be dealing with the case and how much their hourly charge out rates are. A solicitor has a duty to keep a client informed as to the level of costs and of any changes in the charge out rates so that the client is fully aware of his costs position at all times. If the matter is likely to proceed to a contested hearing, the solicitor should provide the client with an estimate of costs and include the barrister's costs in that estimate.

Payment of costs

The client is responsible for payment of his solicitor's bills for the work carried out on his behalf. A bill should include a summary of the work undertaken. It will set out the solicitor's costs and stipulate the period of time these costs cover. The solicitor's costs are profit costs and disbursements. Profit costs mean all the chargeable time spent on the file during the period of the invoice and are subject to VAT. Disbursements are the other expenses the solicitor has incurred on the client's behalf. Some disbursements are subject to VAT such as counsel's fees, telephone, postage and copying. Some disbursements do not attract VAT including court fees and oath fees.

Costs queries

Bills are to be paid within 30 days of an invoice otherwise interest becomes payable. A client can request a breakdown of the bill and if he wants to challenge a bill he may do so. The back of the invoice will explain what to do if he does not accept the bill.

Different considerations apply as to whether the case involved court proceedings or not. If not and the bill has not been paid, within one month a client could ask his solicitor to apply for what is known as a Remuneration Certificate from the Law Society.

This is a certificate stating that in the opinion of the Law Society the sum charged is fair and reasonable or, as the case may be, what other sum would be fair and reasonable. As well as applying within one month of the bill, a client will have to pay half his costs, VAT and all the expenses. Alternatively, he can write to his solicitor saying that he will pay the whole bill on condition that they obtain a Remuneration Certificate and if this is unacceptable they will have to return the payment. If there have been court proceedings then he could ask for a detailed assessment of his costs. If he is confused about how to proceed he should contact the Law Society and/or Supreme Court Taxing Office. The Office of Supervision of Solicitors at the Law Society will be able to provide helpful guidance.

When a party instructs a solicitor to act for him it is known as the 'solicitor/client retainer' but he can terminate the retainer by giving written instructions to his solicitor at any time. The solicitor can terminate the retainer only with good reason and on giving reasonable notice. Until a client's costs are paid the solicitor is entitled to retain the file of papers. This is known as a 'lien' on the file.

The terms of business letter should set out whom a client should contact in the event of a complaint.

Orders for costs & wasted costs orders

It is not usual for a costs order to be made in children's proceedings. Consideration of all the factors will generally lead the court to conclude that there should be no order.

If a legal representative has acted improperly, unreasonably or negligently and thereby caused a party to incur unnecessary costs it might be appropriate for the court to order the legal representatives to compensate the party for all or part of those costs, by making a wasted costs order against the firm.

Public funding

If a client is funding the case himself, he is a private client, but if a client cannot afford to fund his costs he may be entitled to public funding. Legal Services Commission (LSC) funded services are only provided by solicitors who have a contract with the LSC. For family work the contract must actually cover the specific type of case. A client will need to give full details of his finances to his solicitor for them to assess his financial eligibility. He has to show that his capital AND income are within the current financial limits and these change on an annual basis. Consideration also has to be given to whether the Applicant will benefit sufficiently from the application to justify the likely costs. In contact cases this means showing that the likely outcome of the case will cause 'a significant improvement in the arrangements for that child or children viewed objectively.'

Any funding certificate may be limited in terms of the work the solicitor can undertake, and the amount of costs that can be incurred. If the client's position is unreasonable or it is deemed that there is no prospect of the application proceeding then the LSC may decide to withdraw funding. There have been cases where a father's funding certificate has been withdrawn after it was made clear by the CAFCASS officer in the welfare report that his residence application was unmeritorious.

What funding is available in family proceedings?

Approved family help

This covers assistance in resolving a dispute through negotiation or otherwise, including issuing proceedings and representation where necessary to obtain disclosure of information from another party, or to obtain a consent order following an agreement of matters that were in dispute. There are two types available:

- Help with Mediation. This is limited to giving legal advice and assistance to support family mediation. This is only available if a party is taking part in Family Mediation or has successfully reached an agreement or settlement as a result of Family Mediation.
- General Family Help. This is for legal advice and assistance on family matters and to cover negotiations where a party is not attending mediation. Generally it will not be granted unless the suitability of the case for mediation has been considered.

Legal representation

This level of service is so that a party can be represented in court if he is taking or defending court proceedings. This is the same level of service previously called Legal Aid. There are two types available:

- Investigative help. The funding is limited to investigating the strength of a claim.
- Full representation. The funding is provided to represent a party in legal proceedings.

A certificate will not be backdated, but in some cases involving children the solicitor can act immediately. If a case is urgent the solicitor may be able to apply for emergency Legal Representation.

With Legal Representation a party may have to pay a contribution depending upon his financial status and this will be calculated for him. Contributions from income are by way of monthly instalments but contributions from capital have to be paid as soon as he accepts the offer of a certificate.

In terms of the costs a party pays, if he wins this depends on whether the other side is ordered to pay his costs and in fact does so. If he loses, then the most he will normally have to pay towards his solicitor and barrister's costs is his contribution under his certificate. The court will not normally order him to pay his opponent's costs but it may do so depending upon his conduct and will be dependent upon his own financial position.

Current developments affecting publicly funded clients

A consultation paper, *Legal Aid: a sustainable future* was published jointly by the Department of Constitutional Affairs and LSC in July 2006. The paper proposed radical reforms to the legal aid system and, in relation to family work, to introduce fixed and graduated fee schemes to replace hourly rates and tailored fixed fees. *Legal Aid reform: The Way Ahead* was published at the end of November 2006 after a short consultation on the proposals and confirms the move towards fixed and graduated fee schemes in October 2007. There are concerns that vulnerable children will not obtain the specialist legal representation they require because the fees are being squeezed.

On 11 January 2007 in a House of Commons debate the current legal aid Minister Vera Baird said that there would not be any cuts to the family legal aid budget – in 2007 family legal aid expenditure would be more than 20% higher than it was two years ago.

The legal aid debate continues.

Chapter 8
Getting to grips with the basics

Paternity

If the paternity of a child is in dispute and a man wishes to establish whether or not he is the biological father of the child there are a number of statutory provisions which may assist him. We look at these in detail below. There are various reasons why he might be anxious to establish paternity. For example, if he wants to make an application under the Children Act for a parental responsibility order or an order for residence or contact and a dispute as to parentage arises, the court will not make any orders under the Children Act until the paternity dispute is settled. Alternatively, he might want to prove that he is not the biological father of the child: for example, to avoid a potential claim for financial provision for the child.

Starting point

Married fathers
If a man was married to the child's mother when the child was born then there is a presumption that he is the father of the child, and this is so even if by the time the child is born the parties are divorced. This is known as the 'presumption of legitimacy'. The presumption may be rebutted by evidence which shows that it is more probable than not that the child is not the husband's: for example, that the pregnancy was rather too long. The best form of evidence will be that derived from bodily samples, which can be DNA tested. We look at DNA testing below.

Unmarried fathers
If a man was not married to the child's mother there is no such presumption. What about registration of the birth? If his name is on the birth certificate that may be evidence of paternity but that does not prevent the mother from subsequently denying his paternity or he himself denying it. This also applies to married men despite the presumption of legitimacy. There might be a scenario where a man believes he is the father of a child who has been registered as another man's child on the birth certificate. For example, the man was having an affair with the mother around the time she became pregnant. He may decide he wants his name on the birth certificate and needs to know what steps to take to achieve that.

So how does a man establish paternity?

Establishing Paternity

There is no unified statutory procedure for establishing paternity in England & Wales. Which procedure is used will depend upon the circumstances. The standard of proof for establishing paternity is the balance of probability, not proof beyond reasonable doubt.

Application for a declaration of parentage under the Family Law Act 1986

If a declaration of parentage under the Family Law Act 1986 is made, the court notifies the Registrar General who has discretion under the Births & Deaths Registration Act 1953 to re-authorise the re-registration of the child's birth. The original birth certificate is annotated to show the birth has been re-registered.

Is it possible for a man in a scenario like the one looked at above, to make such an application so that the birth certificate will be amended to include details of his paternity?

Under the Family Law Act the child him/herself or one of his/her parents may apply. Anybody else who tries to apply will be prevented by the court from doing so unless the court considers that that person has a 'sufficient personal interest' in the outcome of the application. On this basis the man in our scenario should be able to show to the court that he has a sufficient personal interest in the outcome to be allowed to apply.

Even so, the court may refuse to hear the application if it decides that determining the issue of paternity would not be in the best interests of the child. What about the child's right to know who his/her father is? We look at this further below; but the bottom line is the court will need to strike a balance between the rights of the child, mother and father and in doing so must consider the welfare of the child.

Obtaining a declaration of parentage under the Child Support Act s27

A declaration of paternity can be made under this Act but is only effective for Child Support purposes. In England & Wales if the mother's husband or the unmarried father, whose name appears on the birth certificate, denies paternity the CSA cannot make a maintenance assessment until the issue of paternity has been resolved. The effect of the declaration of paternity is that the 'father' is liable to pay maintenance even if he continues to dispute his paternity. The maintenance is back-dated to the date the mother made her application.

We look at proposed reforms to Child Support in Chapter 17.

Proving Paternity by scientific means

Blood samples and DNA Testing

By far the best way to establish paternity is by means of DNA testing. There have been two important changes to the law which have made it easier to obtain bodily samples for testing and therefore proof of paternity. These are the:

- **Blood Tests (Evidence of Paternity) Amendment Regulations 2001**
  Under the Family Law Reform Act 1969 it was only possible for the court to direct the use of blood tests in order to resolve a dispute about paternity. Thanks to the Blood Tests (Evidence of Paternity) Amendment Regulations 2001, bodily samples other than blood may now be taken. Refusal to take a blood test for religious reasons is no longer a stumbling block now that these Regulations are in place.

- **Child Support, Pensions & Social Security Act 2000**
  The Family Law Reform Act 1969 did not give the court express power to direct the taking of a sample from a child for the purpose of establishing paternity unless the person with care and control of the child, which in the majority of cases is the mother, consented. This caused enormous difficulties. The Family Law Reform Act was amended by the Child Support, Pensions & Social Security Act 2000 to enable the courts to authorize the taking of a sample from the child even when the mother refuses consent, provided the court considers that it is in the best interests of the child concerned.

Can I just apply for the court to order a DNA test?

It is not possible to make a freestanding application for a DNA test – in other words the court will only make a direction for the use of blood tests or bodily samples in the context of existing proceedings, such as under the Children Act for example. It follows on from this that the best option for a man who has good grounds to believe he is the father of a particular child, and where the mother refuses to acknowledge his paternity, is to make an application under the Children Act. It is not unknown for a mother to react to the 'father's' application for parental responsibility or contact or residence by denying that he is the father of her child. Since the issue of paternity will have to be determined before the application under the Children Act can proceed, at least the matter will be before the court.

How will the court approach the case?

The court has discretion to refuse direct testing and even to hear the issue of paternity at all. However, where paternity is a major factor in the case the court is unlikely to refuse to hear the application. The court could refuse to direct a test if it is not in the child's interests. That being said, it is almost always in the interests of justice to establish the truth and for the child to know the true identity of his/her father. DNA testing is the most reliable means possible of proving that.

My ex won't give a sample for DNA testing. What can the court do?

In civil proceedings the courts cannot compel any adult to provide a sample. So an adult male whom the mother alleges is the father of her child may refuse to provide one. The Child Support, Pensions & Social Security Act 2000 makes it clear that samples may not be taken from anyone other than the child except with his or her consent. Consent is required from an adult before DNA testing may be undertaken.

Nevertheless, if the court has made a direction for tests and an adult party refuses to provide a sample so that a test may be carried out, the court can draw inferences as to why the test was refused. For example, if a mother alleges that a man is the natural father of her child and he denies it, but then chooses to exercise his right not to consent to being tested, then the court may well draw the conclusion that he is the father of the child. Drawing adverse inferences is not ideal but it does sometimes have the effect of encouraging a party to take a test.

The child's right to know who the biological father is

Most courts have taken the view that it is generally in the best interests of a child to know who his/her biological father is. The Adoption & Children Act 2002 gives an adult who has been adopted some right of access to his original birth certificate, and in a case before the European Court of Human Rights it was recognised that everyone should be able to establish details of their identity. The general consensus seems to be that it is important for a child to know about his/her origins. We look at the whole issue of Human Rights in Chapter 17.

Can a paternity case be re-opened now that DNA is available?

A recent case before the European Court of Human Rights concerned a married father who had disputed the child's paternity since the child's birth but to whom DNA tests were unavailable at that time. A blood test was directed but the result was not conclusive and he was unable to disprove his paternity and rebut the presumption of legitimacy. Later when DNA testing became available he was able to establish conclusively that he was not the father, but the court would not reopen the proceedings on the basis that scientific progress could not be used as a ground for so doing. The European Court of Human Rights said this was not the right approach because a balance had to be struck between protecting the legal certainty of relationships and the husband's right to have the legal presumption of legitimacy reviewed in light of the DNA evidence. The domestic court should interpret existing legislation in light of scientific advances.

Who's the father now? Altering the legal status

There are certain circumstances where the status of fatherhood will be transferred from someone who is the biological father to someone who is not the biological father by statute. For example, under the Human Fertilisation & Embryology Act 1990 as follows:

- When a man consents to his sperm being donated for the purpose of licensed fertility treatment, he will not be treated as the father of the child.
- If a married woman has IVF treatment and the sperm which is used to fertilize her eggs is not her husband's, he will still be treated as the father of her child unless it is shown that he did not consent to the IVF treatment.
- If an unmarried woman and man receive licensed fertility treatment and the sperm which is used to fertilize her eggs is not his, for him to be classified as the father of her child the parties must be treated together. In practice this means that if the parties separate before the eggs are implanted into the mother and her partner withdraws his consent to the treatment, then his original consent to treatment is no longer valid because they are no longer together.

Adoption also has the effect of transferring the status of fatherhood from the biological father to the adoptive one.

Does biology matter?

The 1990 Human Fertilization & Embryology Act states that before offering anyone treatment a fertility clinic must take account of the needs of the child to have a father. The importance of a father is made clear. Under proposed rule changes fertility clinics will no longer have to consider a baby's need for a father and single women and lesbian couples will now be entitled to IVF treatment on the NHS. So does biology matter?

In a recent case[1] the children were born by anonymous sperm donation to a lesbian couple. They split up and the High Court made a shared residence order to enable the non-biological mother to achieve parental responsibility and an order prohibiting the biological mother from moving any significant distance away. She flouted the order and the Court of Appeal then awarded residence to the non-biological mother and stated that the biological parent cannot take precedence over the other parent, and that children's views as to whom their psychological parents were should be taken into account. According to the Court of Appeal, when deciding such disputes 'blood ties' were no longer deemed an advantage when both parents had cared for the children. This was a rather worrying decision for a natural father.

The case was appealed to the House of Lords who said that the unusual scenario had distracted the lower courts from the principles of universal application. While not raising a presumption in her favour, the fact of biological parentage was an important and significant factor in determining what would be best for the children, and a child should not be removed from the primary care of his/her biological parents without compelling reason. So, according to this judgment, biology does still matter.

Concern has been raised over the legal status of various categories of 'parent' following this decision, such as a non-biological lesbian parent as in this case, or parties who use a surrogate mother to have a child. And what about sperm donors? We considered the situation under the Human Fertilisation & Embryology Act 1990 where the sperm is donated by a stranger for the purpose of licensed fertility treatment, but what about where the sperm donor is known to the parties? This is important because with fewer men donating their sperm to sperm banks there are more cases where lesbian couples ask someone they know to donate sperm to enable them to have a child.

All parties should consider the legal implications of such action. Once the child is born the known donor could apply for parental responsibility – which we look at in the next section – or even contact. The lesbian couple need to bear that in mind. In view of the House of Lords decision the court is likely to support the right of the father to be involved with the child born to the lesbian couple if he were so minded to make an application to it for parental responsibility.

---

1 Re G (Children 2006 UKHL 43)

Parental responsibility

Meaning

The Children Act defines this as 'all the rights, duties, powers, responsibilities and authority which by law a parent of a child has in relation to the child and his property'. It means having the responsibility for taking all the important decisions in the children's lives relating to their day to day care, religion, education, and medical care. The emphasis is on 'responsibilities' towards the children and not rights over them. Parental responsibility is to be exercised for the benefit of the child not the parent. The duties involved in parental responsibility will change from time to time depending upon the age and maturity of the child.

Married fathers and parental responsibility

If the father was married to the child's mother at the time of the birth then he will have parental responsibility automatically. Married parents both have 'joint' parental responsibility.

Unmarried fathers and parental responsibility

So far as the biological unmarried father is concerned he will not have automatic parental responsibility, but since December 2003, as a result of an amendment to the Children Act by the Adoption & Children Act 2002, provided he registers his children's birth jointly with the mother he will obtain it.

The amendments to the Children Act by the Adoption & Children Act are now enabling more unmarried fathers to acquire parental responsibility; but not all unmarried fathers will be covered under the new law therefore it is necessary to consider the other ways to acquire it.

For an unmarried father who has registered his children's birth prior to the implementation of the new provisions or has not registered the birth of the children jointly with the mother, he can still acquire parental responsibility as follows:

- By entering into a parental responsibility agreement with the mother. This must be on a prescribed court form. An agreement may be terminated by order of the court either on an application of a person with parental responsibility, or with leave of the court, on an application by a child with sufficient understanding.
- By applying to the court for a parental responsibility order. We saw in Chapter 6 that this is one of the five main private law orders made under the Children Act. The court will look at the degree of commitment which he has shown towards his child; the degree of attachment which he has shown and which exists between him and his child; and his reasons for applying for the order. If he satisfies the test, the presumption is that a parental responsibility order should be made. Where a father has shown himself willing and anxious to pick up the responsibility of fatherhood, then the law should give him

parental responsibility. At all times the welfare of the child must be the court's paramount consideration.

- By being appointed a guardian either by the mother or the court. Note, however, that he will assume parental responsibility only in the event of the mother's death.
- By obtaining a residence order from the court. This automatically gives him parental responsibility. We will look at residence applications later.
- By marrying the mother.

Stepfathers and parental responsibility

There may be a situation where the mother has children from a previous relationship and remarries. Her new husband treats the children as his. They are children of the family. However, marrying the mother does not automatically give a stepfather parental responsibility, unlike the natural father.

What are the ways a stepfather can acquire parental responsibility?
Prior to the amendments made by the Adoption & Children Act 2002 he could do this in three ways by:

- Being appointed guardian to care for the child if the natural parent dies.
- Obtaining a residence order stating that the child lives with him. If he is married to the child's mother and the child has been living with him for 3 years or more, or he has the consent of everyone with parental responsibility, he has a right to apply for an order. However, it is unlikely that the natural father would consent.
- Adopting the child.

The Adoption & Children Act 2002 amended the Children Act to insert a new section in respect of the acquisition of parental responsibility by stepparents. This provides that a stepfather will be able to acquire parental responsibility in other ways as follows:

- If he is married to the mother, and she agrees to him having parental responsibility, provided the natural father also agrees (where he has parental responsibility), he can then enter into a parental responsibility agreement.
- He can make an application to the court himself as a stepparent for a parental responsibility order.

Limitations
As set out above, if a stepfather obtains a residence order then he will only have parental responsibility for as long as that order is in force. Parental responsibility does not give a stepfather the right to consent – or refuse to consent – to the making of adoption orders in respect of the child, or the right to remove the child from the jurisdiction. In all other respects he will have the same parental responsibility for the child as the natural father.

Civil Partners and parental responsibility

There is also a scenario where one of the partners in a single sex relationship already has children and the other partner plays a significant role in those children's upbringing. The Civil Partnership Act 2004 came into force on 5 December 2005. The Act enables two same-sex individuals who are not close relatives to obtain legal recognition of their relationship by registering a civil partnership provided each is over 18 and neither is married nor in an existing civil partnership. The formation of a civil partnership creates rights and responsibilities. A registered partner can now acquire parental responsibility of his/her civil partner's child in the same way as a stepparent by:

- Agreement between the parent (and any other parent who also has parental responsibility) and the civil partner in which case the civil partner can enter into a parental responsibility agreement.
- Making an application to the court for a parental responsibility order.

Is parental responsibility really necessary?

For a father parental responsibility enables him to be involved in the day to day decision-making relating to his children but for an unmarried father, who does not acquire it automatically, but who wants to be involved, this is a big issue. For example, without it he may have difficulty obtaining information about his children from their school or doctor. For an unmarried father, who lived with the mother and was involved in the day to day care and decision-making relating to their child, it can be a rude awakening to find that without parental responsibility he is not in a position to question the upbringing of his child. There are situations where parental responsibility is absolutely necessary for the unmarried father:

- In the case of adoption; without parental responsibility his consent will not be required.
- If there is a residence order in force and the mother wants to change the child's surname; she does not need his consent if he does not have parental responsibility.
- In the case of abduction; there have been difficulties where unmarried fathers without parental responsibility have applied for a child to be returned under the Hague Convention as it is not clear whether there has been a breach of a 'right of custody' within the meaning of the Convention. Parental responsibility is considered sufficient to establish a right of custody.

Exercising parental responsibility

Common sense dictates that where both parents have parental responsibility they should consult with each other and not take important steps unilaterally. In practical terms, when the parents live apart it is the parent with whom the child lives who normally carries the responsibility for day to day decisions.

As explained in the previous section, in some situations the consent of more than one person with parental responsibility will be required. Where parents disagree about an important issue the court will have to decide the issue for them.

We look at specific issue orders and prohibited steps orders in detail in Chapter15.

In some circumstances it might be necessary to make the child a ward of Court. This means that no major decision relating to the child's welfare may be made without the consent of the High Court.

Can a father apply for a parental responsibility order where his child was not born in the UK and does not reside here?

Irrespective of whether the child is resident here or was not born in the UK, it is possible to obtain a parental responsibility order.

Can a father lose parental responsibility?

He will not lose it due to someone else obtaining it. This is because, as indicated above, more than one person is allowed to have parental responsibility. In fact, there is no limit to the number of people who may have parental responsibility at any one time. But he can lose parental responsibility in the following circumstances:

- The natural father will lose it on death or if his child is adopted. Adoption automatically extinguishes parental responsibility.
- An unmarried father who obtained a parental responsibility order could lose it if the court makes an order ending it. For example, if he inflicted serious injury on his child. It could also be revoked on the successful application of another person who has parental responsibilty or, with leave, on an application by the child himself.
- A stepfather who acquired parental responsibility by being granted a residence order will lose it automatically when the residence order terminates. In fact, anyone other than an unmarried father will lose it in these circumstances.

What happens if the father entrusts his children to the care of someone else?

It is not possible to transfer or surrender parental responsibility, but the father can delegate responsibility for a child on a temporary basis. For example, this could be to a school for a school trip or to a nanny or childminder. Temporary carers do not acquire parental responsibility, but may do what is reasonable while the child is in their care for the purpose of safeguarding or promoting the child's welfare. This includes a stepfather who does not have parental responsibility. For example, this could cover emergency medical treatment.

When does parental responsibility come to an end?

Parental responsibility will come to an end as regards any issue in relation to a child's upbringing as soon as the child itself is mature enough to make a decision about that issue. A balance needs to be struck between parental responsibility on the one hand and the wishes of a mature child (having listened to that child's views) on the other.

In terms of children being able to take responsibility for their own actions, it depends what it is they want to do and their age and understanding and therefore this will vary from child to child. The law prescribes certain ages where it deems that the child will have reached a certain level of maturity to do certain things. For example, at the age of 16 a child could:

- Leave school. If a child attains the age of 16 years during the period from 1 September to 31 January, the child may leave school at the end of the spring term following his 16th birthday. In any other case the child may leave school on the Friday before the last Monday in May.
- Marry with parental consent or a guardian's consent or that of the court.
- Endorse his/her consent on a deed poll to evidence a change of name.
- Consent to sexual intercourse.
- Consent to surgical, medical or dental treatment.
- Be sold cigarettes and tobacco – the Government plans to increase the age limit from 16 to 18 from 1 October 2007.
- Ride a motor bike.

At the age of 18 children reach the 'age of majority' and are fully-fledged adults and in the eyes of the law capable of making their own decisions – unless they are mentally handicapped and incapable of making their own decisions, in which case different considerations will apply.

Chapter 9
Formalizing arrangements

Child arrangements for divorcing fathers

The court will not allow a divorce to proceed unless it is satisfied that adequate arrangements have been made for any 'relevant' children. The court will need to be satisfied as to the following:

- Where they are to live.
- With whom they are to live.
- What contact the other parent will have with them.
- Who will be looking after them on a day to day basis.
- What their health is like. If they need special arrangements because they are disabled, the court will want to know that these arrangements have been made.
- What their schooling arrangements are.
- Their maintenance.

It should be borne in mind that exact details may not be known at this time. For example, the home may have to be sold.

What is meant by the term 'relevant children'?

The court will be concerned with any child who was born to the parties, or who has been treated as a child of the family, who is:

- Under 16 or
- Between 16 and 18 and still at college or at school full-time.

These are 'relevant children'. This includes adopted children and stepchildren but does not include foster children.

How does the Court know if the arrangements proposed are adequate?

When parties divorce, the party petitioning for a divorce, that is the Petitioner, will have to file at court the Divorce Petition together with a form known as a 'Statement of Arrangements for Children form'. In this form the Petitioner will set out the proposed arrangements for the children on divorce dealing with all the points upon which the court needs to be satisfied. The proposals will generally be that the children continue to live with the mother but have 'contact' with the father. The judge considers the arrangements for the children at the same time that he considers what is known as directions for trial, that is, at the same time he considers the divorce papers. If he approves the proposed arrangements a notice of satisfaction confirming this will be sent out to the parties.

How will the father find out what arrangements are being proposed?

If the wife is the Petitioner she will lodge her statement of arrangements for children form at court with her petition for divorce. She may agree the content of the form with the father before it is lodged, in which event an agreed form is lodged. A father will worry about committing himself to agreeing to the mother's proposals that he have 'contact', particularly where it is unclear what the exact contact arrangements are and what her definition of contact will be.

If an agreed form is not lodged, her statement of arrangements form will be served on the father with her divorce petition. He will receive what is known as an acknowledgment of service form with the petition. On that form there is a section asking whether he agrees with the petitioner's proposed arrangements for the children. If he does not he can file his own statement of arrangements form.

Agreeing the arrangements does not preclude a father from making an application to the court for an order reviewing those arrangements at a later date. For example, if subsequently problems develop or there is a change in circumstances making the current arrangements unworkable. The court will decide a particular issue at any given time. In other words, the statement of arrangements form is not a binding document.

If the father is the Petitioner this process will be the other way round.

If the judge does not approve the arrangements what will he do?

He may decide:

- He needs further information about the arrangements being proposed. For example, it may not be clear from the form who is looking after the children while the mother is at work.
- There should be an appointment for both parents to see him in Chambers. He may wish to clarify several points with them.
- A Court & Family Reporter should prepare a report about the children. The Reporter will meet with both parents to talk about the proposals and talk to the children too. The report with the Reporter's recommendations will be sent to the court.
- The arrangements proposed should be in the form of a court order because this would be better for the children. An application for an order would then have to be made, but the court will only make an order if it would be better for the children than making no order at all.

Current developments

In Chapter 6 we briefly looked at the changes proposed by the Department of Constitutional Affairs Consultation document Family Procedure Rules – a new procedural code for family proceedings published in August 2006, one of which is to the statement of arrangements form. It is proposed that the form be simplified and shortened to provide the information the court needs for dealing with the issues at the time it is filed such as the child's name, date of birth and gender; whether the child has any health or educational needs; and whether there are or have been previous court proceedings. Completing the current form can be problematic because it requires the parties to put down the proposed living arrangements for the children and that is not always possible because parties do not know where they will be living at such an early stage.

Child arrangements for unmarried fathers

Their position is completely different. When unmarried parties split there are no formal requirements for the children and no statement of arrangements for children form is submitted to the court. The court is not involved and will not be unless an application is made to it to rule on the arrangements.

Child arrangements for Civil Partners

In any proceedings to dissolve a civil partnership where relevant children are involved, the court is required to consider the arrangements for them. In the same way as on divorce the court may direct that dissolution may not be made final until it is satisfied that adequate arrangements have been made for the children.

Deciding whether to make an application to the court

Considering the options

Having tried everything he can to reach an amicable arrangement with his estranged spouse or partner, a father has several options:

- Cave in and accept what he is being offered. In Part I we have looked at the reasons why fathers sometimes do this.
- Continue trying to come to an agreement with the mother without issuing court proceedings. As we saw in Chapter 2, he might try and enlist the support of third parties to help him. Many fathers state that this is only a short-term option. This is because mothers frequently move boundaries and promise to sort out the arrangements, thereby stringing matters out. The issues are not resolved between the parties because, so far as the father is concerned, the mother has no interest in resolving them. The parties may not even be communicating so there is no possibility of mediating and even if they are and they do, if they still cannot resolve the issues between them then the likelihood is that a court application will be made.
- Set out his requests formally, through a solicitor, and still try to reach an amicable agreement. By this stage fathers are generally resigned to having to

issue proceedings. Unfortunately, the very fact that a father might instruct a solicitor to write a letter setting out his concerns and setting out his requests for contact is often enough to put the mother's back up and to inflame the situation. The father is in fact placed in an extremely difficult position; whatever he does he is caught.

- Issue court proceedings. An agreement can still be reached, but most fathers who find themselves in this position state that, as soon as they issue proceedings, mothers refuse to discuss matters as they feel the application is a personal attack upon them. All cases vary, however, and sometimes one party making an application may make the other party sit up and think about the implications of what they are doing and this gives them the impetus to resolve matters. Invariably matters proceed at least several stages before the matter is compromised anyway.

What are the objectives?

What does a father want to achieve and what are his long-term goals? If he is looking for flexibility, a court order will provide him with a rigid timetable to comply with, and any deviations from it may mean further applications to the court. If a mother is presented with a court timetable she may not be willing to consider any changes, telling the father that this is as a result of the court application that he made and he must accept it.

But if contact with his children is being severely limited then he may feel he has nothing to lose by making an application. Here a rigid timetable may be better because at least it would provide him with some contact. The most common question that fathers ask is, 'What is reasonable contact?' What can they expect from the court? We will look at this in Chapter 14.

Furthermore, any decision imposed by the court upon the father is going to be made by a judge who will adjudicate on the evidence put before him/her and how well the case is presented. How a father stands up to giving evidence will impact upon the outcome of the case. A criticism against judges – justified or not – is that they are biased against fathers and detached from reality. One father told me that he was advised not to proceed to court when it was discovered who the judge would be, on the basis that this judge was, as his barrister informed him, anti men and bad-tempered as a result of suffering from arthritis. The whole point is that any control a father has over the decision-making process, in relation to probably one of the biggest decisions to affect his life, is passed to someone who does not know him or his children at all and only has a snapshot of his life. This is the reality no matter how much deliberation and consideration a judge may make over a decision and no matter how experienced that judge is. This is a hard call for fathers when they are relying upon the legal system to assist them.

An awkward case would be where the father has a degree of contact, or may even enjoy regular contact with his children, but seeks more and/or from time to time the mother goes into maternal gatekeeping mode. He may have reached an agreement with her but she chips away at it so that contact visits/times are topped and tailed or chopped about. He may find that she stops communicating with him over a number of the issues affecting the children and 'forgets' to give him information she would normally share with him. For example, she might decide to go away and leave the children with the nanny or the au pair and fail to inform him. In fact, any ongoing change in attitude should be looked at carefully because it can be the prelude to bigger problems. Fathers complain that mothers do not fully appreciate the meaning of joint parental responsibility and resent the fact that a non-resident father with parental responsibility will want to exercise that parental responsibility in relation to the children too. One father complained to me that his former wife held the view that, so far as she was concerned, since she had given birth to their daughter, she alone had parental responsibility. She refused to acknowledge that he did too and failed to consult him about important decisions relating to their daughter's welfare.

Before resorting to legal proceedings a father should find out about the legal process, the extent to which the legal process can help him achieve his goals but also its severe limitations. Many fathers who have been through the process and expended thousands of pounds, often exhausting their assets in the process, have little to show for it. They do not regard the process as 'father friendly' and see the courts as biased against them.

In my view, which I expressed to the Constitutional Affairs Committee in January 2005, it is not so much a gender issue but a parent issue. It is a balance between the 'resident parent' and the 'non-resident parent' irrespective of gender. This is because the non-resident parent, who in the majority of cases is the father, is on the back-foot when it comes to contact applications. The burden of proof is on that non-resident parent to show why contact should be ordered.

The Constitutional Affairs Committee disagreed and concluded that the courts are not consciously biased towards fathers generally or non-resident parents. They felt that delay in the court process exacerbated problems and that if cases could not be settled then the courts should take responsibility for case management and keeping delays to a minimum.

The fact is for fathers the very idea of having to make an application to the court to see their own children, and for a stranger to decide how often they can see them, is the most desperate situation for them. Worst of all they feel totally helpless because, unable to reach an agreement with the mother, they have no choice but to apply to the court.

Chapter 10
Preparing your case for court

Automatic right to make an application or not?

Those with an automatic right to apply for any s8 order

We looked at the five main private law orders that are of particular interest to fathers in Chapter 6 and dealt specifically with parental responsibility in Chapter 8. As for residence, contact, prohibited steps or specific issue orders, a parent has an automatic right to apply for any of these s8 orders, so this includes the natural father married or not. The unmarried father is entitled whether or not he has parental responsibility. This does not include former parents who have had their child adopted.

Those with an automatic right to apply for a residence or contact order

The following persons have an automatic right to apply for a residence or contact order, but if they want to apply for a prohibited steps or specific issue order, then they need the leave of the court, that is the permission of the court, to make the application:

- A stepfather or stepmother who has treated the child as a child of the family.
- A civil partner who has treated the child as a child of the family.
- Any person with whom the child has lived for at least three years out of the last five years.
- Any person who has obtained the consent of all those people whose legal position would be affected, that is, anyone with parental responsibility or anyone with a residence order, or the local authority if the child is in care.

Those who need leave of the court to apply for a s8 order

All other people not within the above catergories require leave to apply for any order. For example, the natural parent of an adopted child would require leave. A child who wants to make his/her own application also falls within this category. In such a situation the court will only grant leave if it is satisfied that the child has sufficient understanding to make the proposed application. We look at applications made by children and their separate representation in Chapter 11. Grandparents and members of the extended family generally fall within this category.

Consideration for Grandparents

In 2005 the Constitutional Affairs Committee's inquiry *Family Justice: the operation of the family courts*, considered whether the requirement for grandparents to obtain leave should be removed. Families need Fathers gave oral evidence to the Committee that 'grandparents should have a legal right to apply for contact without permission.' In my view, which I also expressed to the Committee, where the resident parent does not encourage contact with the non-resident party's parents in many cases it simply does not happen. The Committee recommended that a change should be made in the law to enable grandparents to apply to the court for contact without the need to apply for leave first.

The Government has indicated that it will consider simplifying the process but no promise has been made to remove the need to apply.

Commencing proceedings

Making an application

In practice, if a father has a solicitor acting for him, he/she will deal with the completion of all the necessary forms and send them to him for his approval. For a father acting in person, it is important he knows the procedure particularly as he will almost certainly have to deal with the mother's legal representatives.

Completing the application form

If the father makes the application he is known as the Applicant and the other parties as Respondents. The application form used will either be a C1 or C2. If there are no existing Children Act proceedings then the correct form to use is a C1. If there are existing Children Act proceedings then the correct form to use is the shorter form C2. The application form will ask for details about the child or children in respect of whom he wants to apply for an order, his details, the other parties' details and brief details of the order for which he is applying. He must name as a Respondent every person whom he believes to have parental responsibility. The mother will be a Respondent. If an order has already been made within existing proceedings, he must also name as a Respondent anyone who was a party in those proceedings.

What is Form C1A?

Form C1 and C2 now require the Applicant to tick a Yes or No box about whether he/she believes that the children named in the application 'have suffered or are at risk of suffering any harm from any form of domestic abuse, violence within the household, child abduction, other conduct or behaviour by any person who is or has been involved in caring for the child(ren) or lives with, or has contact with, the child(ren)?' If the Applicant ticks the Yes box then the Applicant needs to complete the supplemental form C1A and set out full details of the incidents. Section 2 of this form is to be used by the Respondent to reply to allegations made by the Applicant.

There has been a good deal of concern that the introduction of this question will pave the way to false allegations being made against fathers as a means of blocking a contact application before it has even started. The Government has indicated that the new form will deter spurious allegations being made because of the degree to which they have to be described on form C1A, while at the same time protecting those at risk – the purpose of these forms is to alert CAFCASS to the possibility of safety issues, to undertake any preliminary 'paper' assessment of risk and advise the court accordingly. We look at the court's approach below.

Tell me about Parenting Plans

When completing form C1 the Applicant will need to confirm if he/she has received a parenting plan booklet, agreed to a parenting plan in which case he/she must include it with the application, or if a parenting plan was agreed and it has broken down to provide an explanation as to what went wrong. So what is this all about?

The parenting plan booklet was originally published in 2002 and a revised edition in March 2006. Its purpose is to provide parents with information as to what sort of arrangements would be considered acceptable but also to help them become aware of difficult issues concerning their children that might arise and to work out how to tackle them. The revised version gives more advice on the benefit to children of having a relationship with both parents and there is heavy emphasis on mediation in the plans.

As is evident from form C1, parents are expected to consider parenting plans when separating. Booklets should be available from the Citizen's Advice Bureau, court offices and CAFCASS. Some parents may find parenting plans helpful. We look at the limitations of these existing parenting plans in Part III.

Issuing & serving the application

The application form is submitted to the court together with sufficient copies for service and the court fee if appropriate. On filing, the court fixes a date for a preliminary hearing or directions appointment. This is known as the First Hearing Dispute Resolution Appointment (FHDRA), see below. Copies of the application must be served on all Respondents at least 14 days before the hearing, together with a notice of proceedings form C6 giving the date of the hearing and a blank acknowledgment of service form C7.

Where a Respondent has a solicitor representing him/her the best way for the Applicant to serve the papers is by sending them first class post to the solicitor's office or by delivering them. Where the Respondent does not have a solicitor representing him/her the Applicant might serve the papers by giving them to the Respondent personally or by sending them by first class post to the Respondent's address. The Applicant could also use a process server to deliver the papers. This is more costly but the advantage is that the process server can prepare a sworn statement to confirm that the Respondent was personally served with the papers. If there are potential problems with service this might be a good idea, because the Applicant must file a statement of service at court setting out how service was effected, that is, when and how. This is because, if the other side fails to come to court, it is necessary to prove to the court that the other party has been given notice of the proceedings and the opportunity to present his/her case to the court and has not been prejudiced in any way.

As well as serving any Respondents, the Applicant needs to be aware that there are sometimes other persons to whom notice must be given so they can decide if they want to apply to be 'joined as a party', that is made a party to the proceedings. Unlike Respondents they only need to be served with a copy of the notice of the proceedings. They are:

- Any person with whom the child is living at the time of the application.
- Any person with whom the child has lived for three years or more prior to the application being made.
- Any person named in a court order or a party to existing proceedings concerning the child.
- If the child is being looked after by social services, but not subject to a care order, the Local Authority looking after the child.

The Respondent must complete the Acknowledgment form within 14 days of service, file it at court and serve a copy on the Applicant.

Tell me about the proceedings

In 2004 the then President of the Family Division, Dame Elizabeth Butler-Sloss, produced her *Private Law Programme for Children* addressing, among other things, the delay it was taking for private cases to be listed and dealt with by the courts. In her *Private Law Programme* she stated that in all cases:

- The FHDRA should be listed before a District Judge between four and six weeks after the issue of the application.
- The parties should be informed about the conciliation system that runs at the court and that the reason why the FHDRA has been fixed is with a view to helping them attempt to resolve the issues between them.
- The parties should be informed about the arrangements at that court (if any) for the requirement for the children to attend court. At the Principal Registry in London for example children of nine years and older (and sometimes younger siblings) must come to court and are interviewed by the CAFCASS officer – the Court & Family Reporter (CFR).
- Full use should be made of in-court conciliation at the FHDRA wherever possible.
- There should be detailed and individually focused case management at the FHDRA to identify the issues that need to be determined and a timetable for the case.
- If a direction is made for a CAFCASS report it should be limited to the identified issues.
- There should be judicial continuity throughout the case and of CAFCASS practitioners where possible.
- Urgent applications are to be heard by the allocated judge within ten working days at any stage of the proceedings, including following up the outcome of court orders in appropriate cases.

The approach of the court at the First Hearing Dispute Resolution Appointment 'FHDRA'

Taking account of the Private Law Programme the approach of the court at the FHDRA will be to:

- Investigate the issues.
- Use the first appointment as a conciliation appointment to encourage the parties, if at all possible, to agree the issues between them with the assistance of the court.
- Give directions for the way the case is to proceed if the parties fail to reach an agreement.

What does 'investigating the issues' mean?

If one parent has raised safety issues, for example violence or child abuse, and filed form C1A, then the court must decide at the FHDRA what the issues are and whether a 'finding of fact' hearing is necessary – that is a hearing to assess whether there is any factual evidence to substantiate the allegations being made. What is important is that any findings are made quickly to avoid possible delay and to keep the case progressing, and moreover, if the allegations are found not to be genuine removing the possibility of the errant parent using them as a means to frustrate contact. Having said that, even if the allegations are found proved, there is no presumption against contact although there are likely to be conditions attached to any contact order made. It cannot be emphasized enough the importance of the court getting it right and there needs to be a balance between speed and a thorough investigation of the allegations for the sake of everyone concerned.

Conciliation

If there are no safety issues and in-court conciliation is available then the parties should be able to take advantage of it. So far as conciliation court schemes are concerned, there is no uniform system and, although there are schemes in operation at divorce county courts and family proceedings courts, as indicated above, there are variations amongst the courts. The Principal Registry in London runs a conciliation scheme that deals with children's issues. When an application is issued, the conciliation appointment takes place before a District Judge sitting with the Court & Family Reporter (CFR). The parties will be present as will their legal advisors. They will be encouraged to settle their dispute by negotiation.

Conciliation appointments are confidential and informal. An order cannot be imposed upon the parties. If the children are attending then the CFR will speak to them independently out of court and their views will then be discussed in court with the parents. Both the District Judge and the CFR should offer suggestions and it is exceptionally helpful if the District Judge gives some firm guidance to the parties as to the likely outcome of the application as this helps to focus their minds. Sometimes a series of conciliation appointments is used to progress contact. Neither the judge nor the CFR at the conciliation appointment will take any further part in the proceedings.

The appointment can also be adjourned so that parties can attend mediation sessions. In addition to conciliation at court, CAFCASS offers mediation away from court. Following receipt of a referral from the court, CAFCASS should contact the family within five working days, provide them with information about the mediation process and offer an appointment within three weeks of the referral.

If no agreement is reached, directions will be given as to how the case should proceed.

Directions
The court will make a number of different directions dealing with the timing of cases, admission of evidence and administration matters for example. We look at these in detail below.

What directions might the court make?

The directions made will vary depending on the case before the court. It is important that the directions given are tailored to the particular case.

Timetabling the case
The court may direct that there be a timetable setting out the dates by which certain things need to be done and to which all parties must adhere. The courts are conscious of delay in children's cases. Delay is one of the major criticisms of the court system. We have already touched on the no-delay principle in Chapter 6.

Welfare reports
S7 of the Children Act deals with welfare reports. A report is not ordered in every case, but where the court feels it needs one to assist it to make its decision. It will be prepared either by the Court & Family Reporter (CFR) employed by CAFCASS or by the Social Services Department of the Local Authority. Most reports are prepared by CFRs. Social Services are usually only involved where the children who are the subject of the application are already known to them. The CFR will see the court file and interview both parents and the children. The CFR will want to see how both parents interact with the children and therefore to see each parent alone with the children in a home environment.

CFR's might also interview schoolteachers, the family doctor or grandparents, if their views are relevant. The report will then be prepared and generally this includes conclusions and recommendations about which order would be appropriate for the court to make. The report carries a lot of weight with the court. For the most part these statements are very conservative in their approach and there has been a lot of criticism that they are heavily weighted in favour of mothers. Many fathers complain that they do not have the opportunity to challenge the report in court. If they want the CFR to attend to give evidence and for cross-examination they have to ask the court to make an order for the CFR's attendance.

s37 reports
A s37 report is not to be confused with a s7 welfare report. If the court believes that a child is suffering significant harm in the resident parent's care and that an

assessment of the kind needed could only take place if the child were not in his/her own home, it may be appropriate for a care or supervision order to be made in respect of that child. The court has the power to make a direction for the Local Authority to carry out a s37 investigation into that child's circumstances. The Local Authority will provide a report even if it does not decide to apply to take the child into care. The question is what would the court consider to be significant harm in this context?

In an extreme case, for example, where not only has the resident parent been implacable to contact but has also made allegations of abuse which have subsequently been found to have no foundation, and it is believed that the children are being manipulated emotionally because of the resident parent's false and distorted beliefs about the other parent, the court might order a s37 investigation. Involving the Local Authority and asking them to assess whether it is appropriate to take the children into care even temporarily is an extremely drastic measure but might be justified in such a situation.

Expert evidence

To protect children from unnecessary and repeated medical or psychiatric assessments, these are only allowed if the court gives permission. The court welfare report is generally the preferred step to take, but if there is a particularly difficult medical problem with the child, that will have to be addressed by way of the appropriate expert report. For example, where there have been allegations of sexual abuse, both a paediatrician's expert opinion and a child psychiatrist's expert opinion might be sort.

Wherever possible the expert should be instructed by the parties jointly and this will be the preferred direction of the court. If there is disagreement as to which expert should be instructed then the court needs to address the problem and where possible resolve it. The court should stipulate which documents should be disclosed to the expert.

A meeting attended by a joint expert should normally be with both parties unless they have agreed in writing that this is not necessary. In Children Act proceedings the expert's report must be shown to all the parties, the court and any other expert even if it is unfavourable to the party who instructed the expert. The report cannot be disregarded just because that party does not accept what the expert says.

There has been much concern over 'expert' opinions due to the misdiagnoses of child abuse as for example in the cases of Angela Cannings, Sally Clark and Trupti Patel. The fact that it was sufficient for one expert to claim on the balance of probabilities that the parent was guilty did little to encourage confidence in the legal system.

A court relies on an expert to provide it with independent assistance in relation to matters within his/her expertise by way of an objective, unbiased opinion. The court will be bound by an expert's evidence if it is on a matter solely within the expert's expertise and the judge accepts the evidence is reliable. The court is not bound to follow the recommendations of the expert if it regards the evidence as merely persuasive and not uncontrovertable. He only needs to take it into account and if the judge does not follow it set out reasons for not doing so in his/her judgment. It is therefore a balancing exercise for the court.

An expert is given immunity from being sued in respect of the evidence he/she gives in court but that does not extend to immunity from disciplinary proceedings by his/her professional body. This was confirmed by the Court of Appeal in the GMC case against Sir Roy Meadows. As a result of this and a number of other high profile cases, Professor Liam Donaldson, England's Chief Medical Officer, produced his report *Bearing Good Witness: Proposals for reforming the delivery of medical expert evidence in family law cases* which was published on 30 October 2006. As part of the plan to improve the quality of the medical expert witness it proposes that the NHS establishes teams of specialists doctors and other professionals within local NHS organisations. Junior members of the team will work with senior colleagues and under their supervision, and the responsibility for preparing a medical report for the court and giving evidence in court would be shared between the team members. The aim is to avoid the risk of reports for the courts being biased by the view of a particular individual for example like those of Professor Meadows.

Witness statements

No party may file a witness statement unless the court makes a direction permitting them to do so. Parties generally prefer witness statements to be exchanged at the same time rather than one following on from the other. This avoids tit for tat allegations. Whatever the order made by the court, the court will control the time when this evidence is submitted. The statement is merely the written form of the oral evidence upon which a party intends to rely at court, and upon which the court makes its decision and therefore it must be accurate. Every statement must be signed and dated by the person making it and contain a declaration that he/she believes that it is true and knows that it will be placed before the court.

Limiting disclosure of evidence, reports and documents

All parties to the case are entitled to see all statements which are also seen by the court and the CFR, but in very limited cases the court can order that some documents should not be seen by some or all of the parties. This would only be ordered if the disclosure of the documents would be damaging for the child. We look at the whole issue of confidentiality and disclosure of court documents in Chapter 12.

The children's attendance

The court rules provide that the children must attend all proceedings, but in the children's interest the court can direct otherwise and use its discretion. For example, a very young child would not attend, but at the Principal Registry in London children of 9 years and older would be expected to attend for a conciliation appointment.

Further hearings and hearing dates

Unless the case is resolved, at the end of every court hearing a date must be fixed for the next one. The parties are not supposed to extend any time limit ordered by the court by mutual agreement. This is all part of the no-delay principle and enables the court to retain control of the court timetable. However, it is not uncommon for statements to be late which can become a real problem. See below.

To ensure judicial continuity and continuous case management the judge may reserve the case to himself. This is meritorious but the downside is that sometimes the listing of the case will be delayed because the judge is unavailable. If at the FHDRA the District Judge has directed that a finding of fact hearing is necessary to determine allegations of domestic violence for example, both that hearing and the final hearing must take place before the same judge.

The court will also consider what directions should be given for the attendance of witnesses and the CFR at the final hearing.

The final hearing

The final hearing will be scheduled to take place after any welfare report and any other evidence such as an expert's report and witness statements have been filed. This is why it is important that evidence is filed on time and why the court sets a timetable in the first place. Unfortunately, all too often statements are not filed on time which means hearings get adjourned thereby leading to extra delay.

It is the duty of the Applicant to prepare and file an agreed and paginated bundle of documents two days prior to any hearing which is listed for half a day or more, or any other time specified by the judge. Chronologies, indexes, position statements of both parties including a summary of the order or directions sought by each party at the hearing must be filed one day before the hearing. This is in accordance with the new Practice Direction about bundles which came into force on 2 October 2006. So far as litigants in person are concerned special considerations apply. Where the Applicant is a litigant in person and the Respondent is represented by solicitors the responsibility for preparing the court bundle will be with the Respondent's solicitors.

We looked at the procedure at the final hearing in Chapter 6.

Judgment

This must be delivered as soon as possible after the hearing. Any order made must be in writing. Any findings of fact made by the court and the reasons for the decision will be kept on the court file. A copy of the order must be served on each party and on any person with whom the child is living.

Other procedural concerns...

Applying for leave to make a s8 application

The application for leave, should be made on form C2, setting out the reasons for the application. The draft application, should be filed at court with it. For example, a grandparent might make an application for leave to apply for a residence order. His/her draft application for that residence order will be filed at court as the same time.

The court may either grant the application for leave on reviewing the papers or fix a date for a hearing, in which case it will give directions about who needs to be notified.

We look at applications for leave in respect of children in the next chapter. So far as any other person is concerned, when the court is considering granting leave the welfare checklist (see below) will not apply and the child's welfare is not the paramount consideration. It will have regard to:

- The nature for the proposed application. For example, if the order is for contact is that for direct contact or indirect contact.
- What connection the Applicant has with the child. Biological connections do not guarantee that leave will be given. The court will look at the psychological relationship between Applicant and child. Grandparents generally fall into both categories.
- Whether there is a risk that the proposed application might disrupt the child's life to such a degree that the child will suffer harm, for example, to his/her health or if the child is in care then disruption will be a key factor.
- If the child is in the care of the local authority what plans it has for the child and the wishes and feelings of the child's parents. In one case where the local authority planned to put the child forward for adoption, an aunt was refused leave to apply for residence and/or contact as the mother opposed anyone within her family having contact with the child.

What does it mean to make an application ex parte?

This means to make an application without notice to the other party. For example, it would be used in the case of an emergency where it is anticipated that the other parent intends to abduct the children as that parent has not returned them from a contact visit, or there is an urgent medical problem which needs to be addressed. We look at emergency applications in Chapter 15. If such an application is made, the full application should be filed either at the same time, or served on the Respondent within 48 hours after the making of the ex parte order. Copies of papers read by the judge or any information about what took place, should also be provided to any person served with or given notice of the ex parte order.

The courts do not usually like to make ex parte residence/contact orders without hearing from the other party first. However, it may be possible to obtain an order from the court that the other party only receive short notice, by applying to the court and giving valid reasons why short notice is required. In this way, there will still be an earlier date for the hearing.

Withdrawing the application

Once an application has been issued it may only be withdrawn with the permission of the court. It will be necessary therefore to apply to the court for the matter to be withdrawn.

What factors will the court consider if an application for a s8 order is made?

In Chapter 6 we briefly considered the welfare principle, the 'no order' presumption and the 'no delay' principle:

The welfare principle

This means that when a court determines any question with respect to the:

- Upbringing of the child or
- Administration of the child's property or the application of any income arising from it, the child's welfare shall be the court's paramount consideration.

As we have seen this means the welfare test would not apply where the court is considering an application by a grandparent for leave to apply for a s8 order. That would be a procedural issue and does not involve questions about the child's upbringing unlike the s8 application itself. However, the welfare of the child will still be one of the factors the court will take into account in reaching its decision.

The welfare factors

Before the Children Act came into force the only guidance on how to apply this principle was to be found in the case law. Now the court has a list of seven factors to which it refers when it is applying the welfare principle in contested s8 proceedings. The aim of the checklist is to provide a consistent approach for the courts, the parties and advisors with which to work.

None of these factors is given any priority and the court is left to assess the relative importance of each factor in the circumstances of every case. If a father is applying for a residence order, he needs to show that the children are better off living with him: he will have to consider their physical needs, daily care and routine and see if what he can provide is better for his child, bearing in mind the court does not equate welfare with material wealth or the fact that one parent can offer more.

The checklist is not exhaustive and the court can also take any other relevant factors into account:

- **The ascertainable wishes and feelings of the child concerned (considered in the light of the child's age and understanding).**
  We have already referred to the welfare report and this is one of the ways in which the child's wishes and feelings can be made known to the court. The CAFCASS report should consider the child's wishes, as well as the maturity of the child, and the extent to which the parents may have exerted influence over the child in forming any views. A court is not obliged to follow the suggestions made in the report. We look at situations where a child might be made a party to the proceedings, his/her separate representation, and situations where he/she may give his/her own instructions in detail in Chapter 11.
  A judge may interview a child privately during the case to form his own

opinion, but there does not appear to be any consistency in the approach of judges on this point so the practice varies from court to court. Even if a judge does interview a child to ascertain that's child's wishes, those wishes do not always take precedence and the court may feel that the child's wishes are not in his/her best interests.

Another issue to consider involving a child's welfare is the extent to which a child can consent to or refuse medical treatment. If a child is sufficiently mature he can consent to treatment and only the court can override his consent.

- **The child's physical, emotional and educational needs.**
  This focuses on the child and looks at accommodation, medical needs and education, as well as how close the child is to brothers and sisters and others with whom he may lose touch if a particular order is made. The court considers circumstances very carefully before splitting brothers and sisters. It would be unusual to separate siblings close in age but where there is a large age gap it has happened particularly where the children are already living with a different parent. The court will consider the child's immediate needs and long-term needs and sometimes these will differ.

- **The likely effect on the child of any change in circumstances.**
  If the current arrangements for a child are working satisfactorily, the court will be unlikely to change them. This attitude is often referred to as maintaining the status quo and means the person with whom the child is living, generally the mother, is at a considerable advantage. This is one of the major problems for fathers to overcome because it is very difficult to shift the court from this starting point. Continuity of care is considered as the most important part of a child's sense of security, and disruption of a child's routine is to be avoided if at all possible. The court will look at all changes in the child's circumstances. For example, if another adult is going to be introduced into the child's life because one parent is to remarry or cohabit with someone new or the child is going to have to move to a new home or school.

  Fathers also worry because they know that in most cases the longer the status quo is maintained the harder it is to change it and if there are delays their case will be prejudiced. The philosophy behind the Children Act is that any delay is likely to prejudice the child and therefore a timetable is imposed. Ironically, once proceedings have started this may help, but fathers complain that very often the reason why they issued proceedings was because the mother dragged her feet in sorting out the contact and continually moved the boundary lines.

- **The child's age, sex, background and any characteristics of the child which the court considers relevant.**
  There is no presumption of law that a child of any age should be with one parent or the other but courts invariably order that very young babies live with their mothers. A teenager can generally cope with living with either parent. As seen above, age also has a decisive influence on the importance a court will attach to a child's wishes. If children are from a multi-racial background, then the court will need to look at this background and how they

have been brought up and what influence both parents' culture has had on the children to date. The same applies where the parents come from a different religious background.

- **Any harm that the child has suffered or was at risk of suffering.**
This will cover any past or future harm to the child. Harm is a very broad term and means any ill-treatment of the child or impairment of the child's health or development. Ill-treatment will cover any physical injury such as sexual abuse and psychological injury. Health means physical or mental health, including harm a child has suffered or is at risk of suffering as a result of seeing or hearing the ill-treatment of another person. Development means physical, intellectual, emotional, social or behavioural development.

    The court also considers the harm caused to a child by not seeing both parents. Contact is the right of the child, not of the parent. The child has a right to know his other parent. This is something mothers find very hard to deal with in these circumstances.

- **How capable each of the child's parents, and any other person in relation to whom the court considers the question relevant, is of meeting the child's needs.**
This factor involves the court looking at the parents or other proposed carers to assess their ability to care for the child. The parent's conduct will be relevant to the extent that it may affect their suitability as a parent. If a father has a criminal record that will be a factor the court will consider.

    In disputes between natural parents and another, for example a grandparent, the courts tend to presume that unless there is positive evidence to the contrary it is in the children's best interests to live with their natural parents.

    Whether a parent works will influence the care of the child. The parent's lifestyle and sexual orientation may be relevant. A parent who suffers from mental or physical illness, which could mean sudden or long-term stays in hospital, might also be less suitable as a full-time carer.

    If a parent is proposing to share care with someone else, that person's capabilities will also be considered. This means that new partners or spouses, relatives and friends may be relevant as well as nannies and childminders.

- **The range of powers available to the court under this act and proceedings in question.**
This factor encourages the court to think laterally and to consider every option open to it including that of making no order at all. The court has the power to make any order in favour of any person irrespective of who has applied. For example, in the course of a residence application the court may decide it is better for the child to live with a grandparent even though the grandparent may not have been a party to the application. In s8 proceedings it could also make a family assistance order to provide help to the family from CAFCASS or a local authority. We look at the use of family assistance orders in Chapter 14.

The no-order presumption

As we have seen, the court will not make an order unless it considers that doing so would be better for the child than making no order at all. The reasoning behind this is one of non-intervention and the belief that, in the main, parents know what is right for their children and will act in their best interests.

Where an order would definitely be made

Where there is a real danger that one parent may abduct the child, it would be an advantage to have in operation the restrictions on removal from the UK contained in a residence order.

Avoidance of delay

The court must have regard to the general principle that any delay in determining the question is likely to prejudice the welfare of the child. To a child one year is a long time. A child's sense of time is very different from that of an adult. The court is required to draw up a timetable and give directions to enable it to deal with the matter without delay.

How long will the order last for?

A s8 order will cease to have effect when the child reaches 16, but the court does have power in exceptional circumstances to make or extend an order beyond a child's 16th Birthday. In any event, it will cease when the child reaches 18. If a residence or contact order is made in favour of a parent these orders will automatically end if the child's parents live together for a continuous period of more than 6 months.

Public law

Implications for fathers with children taken into care

Public law is a vast area and relates to the involvement of the local authority and care proceedings. Where there has been violence or abuse, Social Services may need to intervene to protect a child 'at risk'. They have to apply for a court order to do this and to show that the child is likely to suffer 'significant harm' because of the level of care provided at home or because the child is beyond parental control. Social Services might apply for any of the following orders:

- **Care order**
  This is an order to take your child into care;

- **Emergency protection order**
  They need this if they feel the child is in danger and want take the children from your care immediately. They have to go back to court for a care order.

- **Supervision orders**

    If Social Services have a supervision order it means you will be supervised when you care for your children.

    It is not within the scope of this book to deal with public law procedure but it is important to consider these public law orders because of their effect upon a father's contact with a child of his in care.

The local authority has taken the child into care but the father wants contact. Is he entitled?

Contact with the family is in the best interests of a child in care unless proved otherwise. Contact with children in care is subject to the control of the court.

When a care order is made in relation to children, those children should maintain contact with their parents if at all possible. A child in care is afforded reasonable contact with parents, guardians, or anyone with a residence order in force immediately before the care order was made.

If contact is not forthcoming a father could make an application for contact. The application would be made under s34 of the Children Act as it governs public law proceedings, not s8. However, an application can only be made once in every six months, unless the leave of the court is obtained. But if a father is using the application in effect as a means by which he can obtain the return of the child it is unlikely to succeed, especially if the matter has already been fully dealt with by the court.

Although the local authority has a duty to promote contact between the parents and any other person having parental responsibility, it does not have to do so if this is not reasonably practicable or in line with what is in the best interests of the child. The court has to weigh up the pros and cons as to whether continued contact is in the child's best interests. Where a child is in care and an application for contact is made, the court carries out a balancing exercise and weighs up all the factors.

It has been said that contact must not be allowed to destabilize or endanger or frustrate the arrangements planned for the child. The court can require the local authority to justify long-term plans if those plans exclude contact with a parent! The local authority or the child can apply to the court for an order that a 'named' person should have such contact with the child as the court considers appropriate. This includes power to authorize the local authority to refuse contact to a named party.

In exercising its discretion to determine issues related to future contact, the court should have regard to the child's welfare as paramount and to the long-term plans of the authority for the child's future. At the end of the day contact should continue, but it is evident that so far as children in care are concerned there are a number of hurdles to overcome.

The Public Law Protocol came into force on 1 November 2003 for all applications issued by local authorites for care and supervision orders. It was stipulated that the maximum length a case should take is forty weeks and only where there are 'exceptional or unforeseen' circumstances should a case take longer than that. There should also be judicial continuity, active case management by the court, consistency in terms of standardisation of the steps that are to be taken during the process and regular case management conferences.

Special guardianship orders

These orders were introduced by the Adoption & Children Act 2002. If a special guardianship order is made the natural parents retain parental responsibility but it is curtailed so that the special guardian is able to exercise parental responsibility to the exclusion of everyone else. The benefit of the order is that, unlike adoption, ties with the natural family are not severed.

Current Developments

A Government Green Paper, *Care Matters: Transforming the lives of children and young people in care,* was published by the Department of Education and Skills (DfES) on 9 October 2006. Under the proposals, children in care would have the right to choose when they leave care once they reach 16, and measures would be introduced to stop them being repeatedly moved between foster homes; ensure they are placed in the best schools; and provide financial security as they enter adulthood.

Chapter 11
Special considerations for specific categories of litigant

Children and s8 proceedings

In Chapter 10 we looked at the list of welfare factors the court considers when an application is made to it for a s8 order, one of which is the wishes and feelings of the child. In the majority of cases, a child's wishes and feelings will be communicated to the court via the CAFCASS report, but in certain cases it may be in the best interests of a child to be joined as a party to the proceedings and to be separately represented.

Joining the child as a party

In 2004 the President of the Family Division offered guidance on when a child might be joined as a party to the proceedings, indicating that such an order should only be made in a minority of cases involving issues of significant difficulty and that other alternatives such as asking CAFCASS to carry out further assessments or obtaining expert evidence should be considered first.

In all cases, when a CAFCASS officer is preparing a welfare report he/she is under an express duty to consider whether it is in the best interests of the child to be joined as a party and, if so, should notify the court and give reasons why he/she believes joining the child as a party is necessary. In making its order the court will consider the risk of delay. A decision about joining a child as a party should be made as soon as possible.

Here are some examples of situations which **might** justify such an order:

- Where the dispute over residence or contact is intractable.
- Where there is implacable hostility to contact on the part of the resident parent which is unfounded.
- Where the child is suffering harm because of either the intractable residence/contact dispute or the resident parent's unfounded hostility to contact taking place.
- Where the child's views or interests cannot be met effectively through the CAFCASS report. For example, there might be complex or medical health issues involved or allegations of abuse or domestic violence which cannot be resolved through the CAFCASS officer's intervention.
- Where the child is an older child who is objecting to a course of action.
- Where the child has a certain viewpoint and interests which are inconsistent with or incapable of being represented by any of the adult parties.

When a child is joined as a party to the proceedings unless the court is satisfied that the child is able, having regard to his/her understanding, to give instructions in relation to the proceedings[2] that child will need to be represented. If the child is the Applicant he/she will be represented by an adult who acts as his/her next friend and, if the child is the Respondent, by an adult who act as his/her guardian ad litem. The guardian/next friend will instruct a solicitor to act for the child .[3]

The child as a party with a guardian or next friend

A CAFCASS officer will usually be appointed by the court as the child's guardian or next friend. The court makes an order simply stating that CAFCASS has been appointed[4] and CAFCASS will then allocate an officer to the case. The CAFCASS officer will speak to the child and find out what he/she wants and work in conjunction with the solicitor he/she appoints. Sometimes CAFCASS appoints someone from CAFCASS legal in which case it is unnecessary to instruct a solicitor. If CAFCASS is unable to appoint someone without delay, the court may appoint an officer from the National Youth Advocacy Service (NYAS). This is a 'not for profit' children's charity and one of the things it offers is advocacy services to children.

The guardian/next friend is the person who reads the court papers, goes to court hearings, prepares statements on behalf of the child and gives oral evidence. It is his/her task to decide on the child's behalf what is in the child's best interests as well as informing the court about the child's wishes.

The child as a party without a guardian/next friend

A child will need the permission of the court if he/she wants to apply for a s8 order him/herself and this will be given only if the court is satisfied that the child has sufficient understanding to make the application. The application will be for leave to apply and must be dealt with by the High Court.

The child does not have to have a guardian/next friend if the solicitor acting for him/her considers the child is able to give instructions in relation to the proceedings and the judge accepts the solicitor's recommendations. If subsequently the solicitor forms the view that the child is no longer able to give instructions then he/she must inform the court immediately for the court to consider the appointment of a guardian/next friend. The court itself may revoke any permission it gave for the child to act without a guardian/next friend if it considers the child does not have sufficient understanding to continue.

Recently the Court of Appeal recognised that in the case of articulate teenagers the courts must accept that their right to freedom of expression and participation in proceedings outweighs the paternalistic view that the child should be represented by a guardian whose role is to advocate that child's welfare.[5] This ties in with Article 12 of the UN Convention on the Rights of the Child 1989 which requires that a child who is capable of forming his own views has the right to

---

2 Rule 9.2A of the Family Proceedings Rules 1991 (as amended)
3 Rule 9.2 of the Family Proceedings Rules 1991 (as amended)
4 Rule 9.5 of the Family Proceedings Rule 1991 (as amended)
5 Mabon v Mabon [2005] EWCA Civ 634 [2005] 2 FLR 1011

express those views freely in all matters affecting him and to be taken seriously. Article 13 accords a child the right to freedom of expression. In light of the Court of Appeal's judgment it is more likely that older children will be allowed to act as a party without a guardian/next friend.

Current developments

Unlike in public law proceedings, a child in s8 private law proceedings will only be a party to the proceedings and entitled to separate representation if an order is made by the court to join the child as a party. S122 of the Adoption & Children Act 2002 amended the Children Act 1989 to allow court rules to be made to provide for a child to be separately represented in **all** s8 private law proceedings by making such cases 'specified proceedings' in line with public law. However, in its consultation paper *Separate Representation of Children* published on 1 September 2006 by the Department of Constitutional Affairs, the Government confirmed that it does not support the extension of separate representation to all children in all s8 private law proceedings.

What the Government proposes is to establish new rules so that where separate representation is needed it is provided in a timely and appropriate way. It is proposed that all levels of court will have authority both to decide if a child is to be made a party and to hear applications by a child rather than refer them to the High Court as is the current position. This would help reduce stress, delay and promote continuity.

The Government recognises there should be better management of cases; intractable and complex cases need to be identified earlier, and children should be provided with better support and information with a view to avoiding unnecessary anxiety and uncertainty.

While it is agreed and accepted that giving the child party status and separate representation is most beneficial in intractable cases because it enables parents to refocus attention on the child, there is also concern that bringing a child into proceedings can be stressful and puts too much responsibility on the child. It is the current view of the Government that separate representation would be inappropriate in many cases.

Litigants in person

A father may find that he has insufficient funds to pay legal fees but is still ineligible for public funding and has no alternative but to act as a litigant in person. Fathers often start out with legal representation but end up as litigants in person due to prohibitive legal costs. Some fathers may even decide that they are better off presenting their own case so might as well act in person. As one father put it, 'Why should I pay my lawyers tens of thousands of pounds to put my case a tenth as well as I could put it myself?' His representatives would no doubt disagree, but whatever the reason for becoming a litigant in person it is clear that more and more fathers are making a conscious decision to represent themselves, often with the assistance of a McKenzie friend.

What is a McKenzie friend?

The title McKenzie friend comes from a 1970 case of that name, but the role a McKenzie friend has to play was recognised as far back as 1831 in a case where it was noted that any person may:

- Attend as a friend of either party.
- Take notes.
- Quietly make suggestions.
- Give advice.

Litigants in person can often find the whole court process daunting and overwhelming especially when dealing with legal professionals. The presence of a McKenzie friend is therefore an invaluable support, but in order for a McKenzie friend to sit in on court proceedings the judge has to permit him/her to do so. This has caused problems in the past due to the inconsistent approach taken by judges about whether to permit a McKenzie friend to sit in or not, a fact which was recognised by the Court of Appeal in a recent case.[6] The court considered the circumstances where a McKenzie friend should be permitted to sit in on the proceedings and the documents which can be disclosed to a McKenzie friend and offered guidance on both. Guidance on McKenzie friends was also issued by the Office of the President of the Family Division in 2005. The current position is as follows:

McKenzie friends and court proceedings

- There is a presumption in favour of allowing a McKenzie friend to sit in on court proceedings to assist the litigant in person by prompting, taking notes and quietly giving advice.
- This ties in with Article 6 of the European Convention on Human Rights which directs that those who need assistance with the presentation of their case should receive it.
- The assistance does not extend to conducting litigation or acting as an advocate, although in exceptional cases where a litigant in person is inarticulate and unable to present his case some judges have allowed McKenzie friends to address the court directly.
- If a litigant in person requires the assistance of a McKenzie friend he should raise the issue as soon as possible. The sooner he does so the quicker he can obtain the approval of the court for that assistance.
- While the application is made to the court to request the McKenzie friend's assistance it is good practice for him/her to be present in court. He may need to be there anyway to assist the litigant in person with the application. Furthermore, from the judge's point of view he can satisfy himself that the McKenzie friend understands his role and the requirement to maintain confidentiality.
- It might be helpful for the McKenzie friend to produce a short statement about himself confirming that he has no personal interest in the case and that he

---

6 O'Connell & Ors (Children) Rev 2 [2005] EWCA Civ 759

understands the role of a McKenzie friend and the court's rules as to confidentiality.

- Once the judge has given his approval the McKenzie friend will be able to offer the litigant in person assistance. He should bear in mind though that if he wastes time by unnecessary prompting or delay he may be warned by the court and if he persists his permission to assist may be revoked. If his behaviour becomes disruptive in court then he may be excluded from the proceedings.

The documents which may be disclosed to a McKenzie friend

We look at the prohibition on disclosure of documents to third parties generally in the next chapter. So far as McKenzie friends are concerned the following considerations apply:

- S12 of the Administration of Justice Act 1960 stipulates that it will be contempt of court to publish any information relating to the proceedings if the proceedings relate to children. There is specific reference in that Act to proceedings issued under the Children Act, brought under the High Court's inherent jurisdiction and generally where there is an issue relating 'wholly or mainly to the maintenance or upbringing of a minor.' However, disclosure to an approved McKenzie friend does not fall foul of the statute and is therefore not prohibited.
- Although it is good practice for a litigant in person to obtain the court's permission before enlisting the assistance of the McKenzie friend, it should not be contempt of court for the litigant in person to seek the McKenzie friend's assistance or to show him court papers before the court has given approval for that particular McKenzie friend to assist. The reality is that the McKenzie friend is going to require knowledge of the case and access to the court documents to be able to assist. In fact, from 31 October 2005 the Family Proceedings Rules rule 10.20A(3) permits a party to disclose any information relating to the proceedings to a lay advisor or McKenzie friend for the purpose of obtaining advice or assistance in relation to the proceedings.
- The McKenzie friend should be aware that access to court documents brings with it the responsibility not to disclose them or to publish the information they contain to any third party without the permission of the court. The word 'publish' is used in the legal sense which includes giving information to friends or relatives as well as to the press.

Other considerations

In Chapter 10 we looked at notice of proceedings and preparation of court bundles where special considerations are given to litigants in person. The Court of Appeal has made it clear that litigants in person are entitled to as fair a hearing as any other litigant and as much courtesy!

If you are acting as a litigant in person bear in mind that if you are not given adequate notice of all applications being made and/or do not receive copies of all relevant documents in time to be able to prepare for the hearing, this might well breach the right to a fair trial. In such circumstances it may well justify any order made being set aside on appeal.

Chapter 12
Disclosure, Confidentiality & Publicity

The rules relating to what must be disclosed to the court by the parties to proceedings involving children and what may not be disclosed and to whom, have caused problems for fathers. Some have found themselves in contempt of court for revealing details or documents relating to their case to third parties. We looked specifically at what might be disclosed to McKenzie friends in Chapter 11. Now we look at the issue more generally.

When disclosure must be made

Where the welfare of a child is the court's paramount consideration, the parties are under a duty to make full and frank disclosure of all matters relevant to the child's welfare and the issues the court must decide. This is so even if what they must disclose could be adverse to their case. For example, where the court has given permission for a report to be obtained that report must be disclosed even if it is disadvantageous. We looked at this in relation to expert reports in Chapter 10.

Rules about what may be disclosed

The general rule in proceedings involving children, as per s12 of the Administration of Justice Act 1960, is that the proceedings are confidential and it is a contempt of court or an offence to disclose them to the public. This covers disclosing details relating to the actual court proceedings and documents forming part of those proceedings which include witness statements and court reports. The reasoning behind the restrictions is that the child's welfare must come first and that the child must not be put at risk of being identified. However, once a case goes to appeal, although anonymised, public reporting of judgments that reveal many identifying features is permitted so the child's identity may be compromised anyway.

There has been a good deal of criticism about the restrictions on disclosure and the secrecy of the family courts. We looked at the problems facing a litigant in person when seeking the assistance of a McKenzie friend in the last chapter, but the restrictions also made it difficult to seek help from prospective witnesses and to complain to professional bodies and MPs. In January 2005 the Constitutional Affairs Committee recommended that parents should be able to seek advice from their constituency MP and make complaints to relevant supervisory bodies.

Consequently both s12 of the Administration of Justice Act 1960 and the Family Proceedings Rules 1991 have been amended to change the rules as to disclosure. There are now a number of exceptions to the general rule depending on whether the proceedings are held in private; the person who is making the disclosure; the person to whom the disclosure is being made; and the purpose of the disclosure.

Changes to the rules of disclosure in proceedings held in private

With the court's permission

If the proceedings are held in private information, including information likely to identify a child or his address or school, may be disclosed by a party where the court has given permission for that disclosure to be made.

Where rule 10.20A(3) of the Family Proceedings Rules 1991 (as amended) applies

Information may also be disclosed if the person to whom the party wishes to disclose it falls within rule 10.20A(3). Under that rule it is permitted for a party to children proceedings held in private to communicate any information relating to those proceedings likely to identify the child or his address or school to:

- A lay advisor or McKenzie friend so as to obtain advice or assistance relating to those proceedings as we saw in Chapter 11.
- His/her spouse, cohabitant or close family member for the purpose of confidential discussions enabling the party to receive support.
- A healthcare professional or a person or body providing counselling services for children to enable the party or any child of the party obtain health care counselling.
- A mediator for the purpose of mediation in relation to the proceedings.
- A person or body responsible for investigating or determining complaints in relation to legal representatives or professional legal advisors – for example, the Office of Supervision of Solicitors – for the purpose of making a complaint in relation to the legal representative or professional legal advisor.

The same rule also permits a party to children proceedings held in private to communicate the text or summary of the whole or part of a judgment given in those proceedings to:

- An elected representative (MP) or peer, to enable the elected representative or peer to give advice, investigate any complaint or raise any question of policy or procedure.
- The General Medical Council (GMC) for the purpose of making a complaint to the GMC.
- A police officer for the purpose of a criminal investigation.
- A member of the Crown Prosecution Service (CPS) to enable the CPS to discharge its functions under any enactment.

The information provided must be confined to the information which the rule permits the party to disclose.

Over recent years the whole question of the 'secrecy' of court proceedings has been challenged more and more and there have been ongoing demands to alter the rules to make the courts more open and for the rules on disclosure to be relaxed. The issue was addressed by the Constitutional Affairs Committee in 2005 in its report and again in a further session in May 2006.

Confidence and Confidentiality: Improving Transparency and Privacy in Family Courts

In a response to the many criticisms of the 'secret system', the above Government consultation paper was published on 11 July 2006. It stipulates that the primary motivation for consulting on the issue of greater openness is to increase public confidence in our courts, but also that confidentiality is essential – those involved in highly sensitive issues must have the benefit of privacy.

The proposals include making changes to attendance and reporting restrictions so that they are consistent across all family proceedings, and to permit the press, on behalf of and for the benefit of the public, to attend proceedings as of right, though allowing the judge to exclude the press where appropriate. Judges would also be given the discretion to relax reporting restrictions in appropriate cases. Members of the public with a particular interest in a case could apply to the court for admittance. The paper also proposes to make adoption proceedings a special case so that there is transparency up until the placement order for adoption is made, but after that the proceedings remain private.

The Consultation has received mixed views. Some think that the public should have greater awareness of what happens in the family courts and the sort of situations children face. Others maintain that secrecy is sometimes justifiable to protect children's privacy, that children themselves shun and hate publicity, and should be protected from public scrutiny.

What about anonymity of children in family proceedings?

In a recent case[7] a father appealed against an injunction restraining him from publishing various matters concerning his daughter until her 18th birthday, and the Court of Appeal considered the question of anonymity of children in family proceedings. The court agreed that although the prohibition on publication contained in the Children Act 1989 prevented identification of children involved in Children Act proceedings while those proceedings are continuing[8], that prohibition ended once the proceedings were concluded. Any entitlement to anonymity after that was dependent on the court conducting a balancing exercise between the child's right to privacy and any competing right to freedom of expression under the European Convention on Human Rights.[9]

However, the Court of Appeal made it clear that even after the conclusion of

7 Clayton v Clayton 2006 EWCA Civ 878

8 s 97(2) Children Act 1989

9 European Convention on Human Rights for the Protection of Human Rights & Fundamental Freedoms 1950

proceedings the court retains its welfare jurisdiction. In other words, if the court is of the view that the child's welfare will be put at risk by the parent making public details of the case which identify the child, it can and will invoke its powers under the Children Act to grant injunctions to prevent that happening. The Court of Appeal also made it clear that while the decision in this case was a greater step towards transparency of court proceedings, it was not dealing with the broader question of whether or not family proceedings should be heard in private or open court.

The question of anonymity for children leads on to the general question of anonymity in all family proceedings. The concern of some is that it is all very well to have sanctions for breaching the rules but it is futile to rely on sanctions because once the anonymity is breached the damage has been done. How is that to be policed?

Greater transparency might be achieved by allowing the judiciary to anonymise and make public their judgments. However, is it in the interests of justice for any member of the authorised press to attend any court hearing? Would parties want the press, their relatives and neighbours in court to hear their own case?

The view expressed by Lord Justice Wall,[10] who was one of the Appeal judges in the above case, is that the press could be given access to family proceedings provided there were clear ground rules about what they could and could not report, namely the extent to which, if at all, they were to be at liberty when reporting the proceedings to identify the parties, and, in particular, the children concerned. A line needs to be drawn between the public interest and the public's curiosity. To guard against the latter he was opposed to allowing members of the public into family proceedings even if there were a judicial discretion to exclude the public in certain circumstances.

Experts

The cases of Angela Cannings, Sally Clark and Trupti Patel involved evidence from one expert – Sir Roy Meadows – and on his say so alone were found guilty of killing their babies. Many feel that the 'secret system' protects these experts and the evidence cannot be challenged properly when it is given in private. There is also the view that it would helpful to be able to look at reported cases and see how experts fared. Others argue that experts might be reluctant to come forward if that were the case.

Bias

The Government asserts that the system is not biased towards the non-resident parent. We looked at this in Chapter 9 and we look at it again in Part III. It is argued that if the court system were opened up then this would quash the myth that bias persists.

---

10 These comments were made by Lord Justice Wall in June 2006 when he gave the Annual Hersham/Levy Memorial Lecture for the Association of Lawyers for Children and following the handing down of the Court of Appeal judgment in Clayton v Clayton 2006 EWCA Civ 878

In another recent Court of Appeal case[11] Lord Justice Wall dismissed two separate applications for permission to appeal by two litigants in person – both fathers had been denied contact to their children. He said that it was in the interests of open justice to discuss these cases, not least to dispel the myth that there was a gender bias in the family court system which operated to deny contact to non-resident fathers. He also said that the press and some parents' pressure groups needed to understand that the reasons fathers in particular failed sometimes to remain in contact with their children was not due to gender bias in the system but their own conduct. While contact did sometimes break down because of the implacable hostility of the mother, in the judge's experience it broke down more often because of the behaviour of the father.

Although Lord Justice Wall was speaking from his own experience, and not for the whole legal profession, his comments have caused considerable debate and concern among devoted fathers whose children have no contact with them due to the implacable hostility of the mother. In Chapter 5 we looked at the issue of maternal gatekeeping and attempts by mothers to sabotage contact for no apparent reason and where the refusal for contact had nothing to do with the behaviour of the father!

---

11 Re B, Re O 2006 EWCA Civ 1199

Chapter 13
Residence

The question of residence

The primary carer

Mothers are still expected to be the primarily responsible parent and to have residence of the children following a divorce or relationship breakdown.

Fathers face a Catch 22 situation when it comes to their residence claims. The fact is that most fathers work full-time and often very long hours, and this is used against them to defeat their claims. It is argued that, from a purely practical point of view, the children should remain with their mother. However, as we looked at in Chapter 1, the family unit is changing and so are arrangements for the care of children.

Although fathers generally have to work to continue to support the family whether the parties are together or apart, there are many mothers who work full-time and the children are cared for by nannies/child minders. What difference would it make if it were the other way round? Could it be argued that if a father does not have to work or could make arrangements for the children to be cared for while he is working that he could succeed in an application for a residence order? As we have seen, a father who is self-employed would be in a very good position to care for the children. What about the scenario where the father is a 'house husband?'

A few years ago a case – heavily reported in the media – related to a 'house husband' who for a considerable period of time had been the primary carer of the children and wanted residence of them. In this case the mother was the breadwinner and had a very lucrative career in the city. The mother decided she wanted to give up her career and take over the full-time care of the two children aged six and three until the younger of the two went to school. In addition to that she wanted to take the children out of their fee-paying London day schools and to move to Linlithgow sending the children to state schools there. By the time the matter came to court the child-care arrangements had changed to shared parenting. The High Court ruled in favour of the mother and consequently the father sought leave to appeal to the Court of Appeal.

It was argued on behalf of the father that the judge had acted on gender discrimination. If the roles had been reversed and it was the father who wanted to give up his position in the City, with the direct consequence that this would create financial hardship for the family, it would certainly not have persuaded the judge to make an order in his favour. The Court of Appeal decided that, on balance, the mother's reasons for giving up work were genuine; she had based her proposals for residence and contact on an in-depth consideration of what would be the best solution for the children and her proposals were actually better for the children than those of the father. The problem for the father was that he had based his proposals on the mother continuing to earn a lucrative wage in the City and, when it was clear that that would no longer be the case, his proposals fell away. Lord Justice Thorpe, one of the Court of Appeal Judges, rejected the submissions made by the father's Counsel. Leave to Appeal was refused by the Court of Appeal.

Fathers' rights organizations were angered at the decision which they regarded as a regressive step for fathers. The case sparked a number of articles in the press about a father's role, and whether a father can be as good as a mother if their roles are reversed. Fortunately, in recent years the courts are finally recognising that many fathers are 'hands-on' fathers and are making more shared residence orders to reflect this. We look at shared residence orders below.

The non-resident father

Fathers say that it is not just the fact that the children live with their mother that causes problems but the attitude that goes with the status of being 'the non-resident parent'. They assert that mothers believe they are more important than fathers, and that fathers are made to feel as if they are second class citizens, lucky even to be allowed to have contact with their children. The term 'non-resident' parent is seen as discriminatory. Because a father does not generally have residence, contact with his children becomes very precious and if the contact is restricted, then it is obvious that he will push for it and will be aggrieved if he is thwarted at every turn.

Applying for residence

There are many cases where the father could press for residence of the children but does not do so as it would mean dragging up undesirable details relating to the mother's past, and because he is advised that an application presented in such terms would not bode well with the court. One father told me he was advised in no uncertain terms by Counsel that dredging up these details would not put him in a favourable light with the court, and since he was unlikely to succeed in his application anyway then he was best to forget it.

In this case the mother was an alcoholic and regularly went off on drinking binges. She was not really capable of looking after the child, a boy aged twelve, whom the father had looked after since he was a baby. The father genuinely wanted his son to live with him because he feared for his safety and considered making a residence application. The father had his own business and was able to devote time to his son's upbringing. The divorce was particularly acrimonious. The father felt it would be in his son's best interests if he had residence, but he did not want his son to be caught in the crossfire and because he was strongly advised 'to forget any thoughts of applying for residence' he did not make the application. Furthermore, he knew his ex-wife would bitterly contest any application and their relationship would deteriorate further. He was in a very difficult position.

At the financial hearing an extremely unfavourable settlement was ordered on the basis that the son was to live with the mother. The assets in the case were tight and the father was effectively left high and dry. The son moved in with his father a few years later and the father is still trying to unravel the financial settlement. Nearly eight years down the line he feels particularly dissatisfied with the way the legal process treated him. There are many fathers like him.

In the majority of cases the question of residence is therefore decided between the parties and no application for an order is made. Nearly all these cases result in the mother obtaining residence.

Considerations for the court

As a residence order is a s8 order the court must consider the welfare principle and the checklist of welfare factors. The court must also consider, in accordance with the 'no-order' principle, whether it is better to make an order than no order at all. If an unmarried father who does not already have parental responsibility is applying for a residence order and the court grants that order, the court will also have to give him parental responsibility.

In situations where the children have been living with the mother since separation, fathers worry that this will go against them. It is true that courts do favour the status quo and clear evidence is required to show that a change of carer is in the children's interests.

It is generally considered in the children's interests for siblings to remain together and there is also a preference for the children to be brought up by a parent rather than a non-parent. However, the welfare of the child may require the residence order to be made in favour of a non-parent where, for example, the child has developed a deep bond with the non-parent – although, as we saw in Chapter 8 the court will be reluctant to separate the biological parent from his/her child.

The court can make an order for interim residence where it has not had time to fully investigate the issues or other matters remain outstanding. For example, until the financial position is resolved the parties living arrangements may be uncertain. Generally, although not always, the status quo will be maintained by an interim order.

Shared residence

Shared residence is not to be confused with shared parenting. Shared parenting means that both parents have responsibility for the children, whereas shared residence means that the children live some of the time with one parent and the rest of the time with the other parent.

The legal position

The Children Act provides for shared residence. It states that a residence order may be made in favour of more than one person at the same time even though they do not live together and that it may specify the periods during which the child is to live in the different households concerned. It could be weekends with one parent and weekdays with the other parent; alternate weeks with each parent or term-time with one parent and holidays with the other, or other arrangements where the child is to spend large amounts of time with each parent. It follows on from this that a shared residence order does not mean that the children will spend half their time with each parent. We look at this below.

In 2002 the Sub-Committee of the Advisory Board on Family Law reviewed the question of shared residence in *Making Contact Work*. While in favour of parents sharing parental responsibility and maximising contact with the non-resident parent, it decided that a move towards shared residence was inappropriate. The justification for this is that where parties live a long way from each other it would be impractical, parents do not always behave rationally and reasonably in the context of parental separation, one parent may need protection from the other and the child the same protection. Therefore recommendations were not made for it to be implemented at that time.

The current legal position is that there is no presumption for the children's time to be shared between the parents equally or otherwise. The issue was re-considered in Parental Separation: Children's Needs and Parents Responsibilities: Next Steps 2005. I myself submitted evidence to the Constitutional Affairs Committee on the point. Unfortunately, the Government was not persuaded that any legislative change to introduce such a presumption would benefit children, nor would it have any significance in practice. We look at this in more detail in Part III.

What fathers want

Fathers want equal treatment. They do not like the term 'non-resident' parent. Many fathers complain that while the parties were together the mother was more than happy for them to share equally in the child care duties and actively encouraged their relationship with the children, but that as soon as the relationship came to an end the rules were changed.

Although there are mothers who do actively encourage contact and who strive with the father to work together for the benefit of the children, this is not the same as having shared residence. Many fathers feel that the mother assumes she has superior rights to the father because she is the mother and may therefore resist the father's equal involvement. They say it's all about being in control.

If the starting point was a presumption of shared care which could only be departed from if there are strong and clear reasons for doing so, then the distinction between the resident and non-resident parent would disappear – as would a lot of the resentment. When mothers have residence fathers feel sidelined and forced to make contact applications and it is soul destroying even if, after months of battling to obtain a contact order, a mother still does not comply to allow the contact to proceed. It is argued that fathers would not need to make repeated applications for contact if a shared residence order was the standard post separation order. In fact, many of the contact problems would fall away. Currently we have contact and conflict.

Attitude of the courts

Traditionally the courts were reluctant to make shared residence orders at all. It was recognized that in some circumstances a shared residence order can reduce the bitterness between the parties, but it was stressed that there would have to be unusual circumstances where it would be of positive benefit to the child. The court could make a shared residence order in unusual but not unnecessarily exceptional circumstances. This could be where the child has a settled home with one parent and substantial contact with the other.

Fortunately there has been a gradual shift over the past decade towards more shared residence orders being made. In a case in 2001 the Court of Appeal held that it is not necessary to demonstrate exceptional circumstances or a positive benefit to the child.[12] It is sufficient to show that the order would be in his/her interests. This may be appropriate where, for example, there has been shared care for a period of time and during that time the child has coped well with the arrangements.

It was made clear though that if there are major unresolved disputes between the parents then a shared residence order would be inappropriate. Since that case however, objections of one parent to shared residence, the proximity between the parents' homes or even unresolved disputes between them have not been absolute bars to such an order being made. That makes sense because if the parents could agree everything between themselves the court would not need to intervene under the Children Act as they would fall within the 'no order' principle.

The Court may decide that the circumstances dictate that the child should make a settled home with one parent because two competing homes would lead to confusion and stress and the child needs the stability of a single home. On the other hand, the court may feel that a shared residence order is necessary to reflect the reality of the father's involvement.

The bottom line is that the decision to make a shared residence order is at the discretion of the court on the specific facts of the particular case, and shared residence, as we have seen above, does not mean equal residence!

What are the implications of a residence order?

The court is given wide powers to attach directions, conditions, incidental and supplementary provisions to a residence order. These might include directing that the non-resident parent be informed about where the child is to be educated, and any medical treatment the child requires where, for example, the parent with whom the child is living has religious objections to blood transfusions.

When a residence order has been made there are two aspects of parental responsibility which are automatically affected. They are name changes and removing a child from the jurisdiction.

Name changes

When children are born it is convention that leads to them being known by the father's surname when the parents are married or living together, and by the

---

12 D v D (Shared Residence Order) 2001 1 FLR 495

mother's name when she is unmarried and living apart from the father. A child's surname may be changed by:

- The parents or those with parental responsibility.
- By the mature child him/herself.
- With leave of the court.
- By adoption of the child.

Where a residence order is in force a child cannot be called by a new surname without either the written consent of every person who has parental responsibility or the leave of the court. Where there is joint parental responsibility the same conditions apply regardless of whether there is a residence order. For example, where one parent informs the school that the child's name should be changed on the school register, the school should not change it unless it has independent evidence that the other parent consents. If the mother wants to change the child's surname she has to obtain the father's permission and if he refuses it she will have to apply to the court.

The court's decision will be based on the welfare principle, and once again the welfare of the child will be the paramount consideration. It has to be in the child's best interests. This is an area where the case law is changing all the time. However, there are some general principles to be followed:

- If the parents are married they both have a power and duty to register their child's name.
- If they are unmarried the mother has the sole duty and power to do so.
- After registration of a child's name, the grant of a residence order obliges any person wishing to change the surname to obtain the leave of the court or the written consent of all those who have parental responsibility.
- In the absence of a residence order, the person wishing to change the surname from that registered has to obtain the relevant written consent of all those who have parental responsibility or the leave of the court by making an application for a specific issue order.
- On any application the welfare of the child is paramount.
- Among the factors to which the court should have regard is the registered surname of the child and the reasons for the registration; for instance, recognition of the biological link with the child's father. Registration is always a relevant and important consideration but it is not in itself decisive.
- Relevant considerations should include factors which could arise in the future as well as the present.
- Reasons given for changing or seeking to change a child's name based on the fact that the child's name is not the same as the parent making the application does not generally carry that much weight.
- The reasons for an earlier unilateral decision to change a child's name might be relevant.
- Any change of circumstances of the child since the original registration might be relevant.
- In the case of a child whose parents were married to each other the fact of the marriage is important and there would have to be strong reasons to change the name from the father's surname if the child was so registered.

- On an application to change the surname of the child where the parents were not married to each other the degree of commitment of the father to the child, the quality of contact if it occurred between father and child, the existence or absence of parental responsibility are all relevant factors to be taken into account.
- The child's wishes are not decisive.

Changing a child's forename does not seem to be restricted in the same way as his/her surname, although if reasons can be shown why it might not be in the child's best interests to change the first name then that might prevent a change.

Removing a child from the jurisdiction

Where a residence order has been made no person may remove the child from the UK without either the written consent of every person who has parental responsibility or leave of the court.

Holidays or short periods

The Children Act allows the person in whose favour a residence order has been made to take the child out of the UK for periods of less than one month without consent. So if the children live with their mother and she has a residence order she can take them abroad as many times as she likes provided each individual trip does not last more than one month.

The father, on the other hand, as the parent without the residence order, needs to seek consent every time he wants to take the children abroad for whatever period. To avoid him having to make repeated applications to the court, at the time the residence order is granted the court can add a direction allowing him to take the children out of the country. If he lives abroad this means that regular trips for his children to stay with him will be permitted, without having to go to the mother every time to request her consent to the trip.

If this proviso is not included and an application to obtain consent has to be made, the court will base its decision on the welfare principle. If a father wants to take his child on holiday abroad then it would not be difficult to persuade the court that this would be in the child's best interests, unless the mother can show that the holiday is being used as a cover for abduction. He would need to make an application with a statement in support to get leave for those dates.

If there is no residence order in force then in theory either party can take their children abroad without any restriction or need for consent. However, the parent proposing the trip could be prevented from taking the children by the other parent obtaining a prohibited steps order forbidding the children being taken abroad if there is a real threat that the other parent does not intend to return them. Additionally, a criminal offence will be committed by the parent or any other person removing the children if the permission of the other parent or the court is not obtained. The offences will be committed under the Child Abduction Act 1984. If there are concerns then the court could require the father to enter a bond -- surety from the bank or another financial institution – on removal from the jurisdiction.

Leaving the country permanently

This is one of the possibilities that fathers dread. Many of the cases involve mothers who have remarried and wish to relocate with their new husband or where the new husband is a foreign national. There are also cases where the mother is a foreign national and after the parties split she wishes to return 'home' to her family. For the mother to do this she will need the consent of all persons holding parental responsibility otherwise she will need to apply for leave to remove the children, in which event she will need to convince the court of the merits of her application.

The court considers the following factors on such an application:

- It will review the welfare checklist. The court does not have to go through every factor but it must direct itself to the list. It will want to know the children's thoughts and feelings on the matter. What have they been told? Do they understand the implications of moving so far away in terms of the contact with their father? Have they been able to talk to him about it? Will they suffer harm as a result of losing contact and if so, is that sufficient reason to refuse the application? The older the child, or the greater the child's special needs at any age, the harder it may be to persuade the court that the child will be better off being uprooted than left in the jurisdiction with the other parent, provided that parent had played a full role in the child's care since separation.

- The leave of the court should not be withheld unless the interests of the child and those of the parent with care are clearly incompatible. Previously the courts held that the mother should be allowed to relocate because she might become unhappy if not allowed to do so and that this might adversely affect the child. But this should only be taken into account if the overall proposal is reasonable.

- Contact. Are the current contact arrangements good or not and will the mother help maintain the contact? How is this going to be maintained? When direct contact cannot take place, what about indirect contact and how much will all this cost? This is a supremely important consideration. Fathers argue that on paper mothers' proposals may seem feasible and workable but that in reality, once the children are abroad, particularly if they are thousands of miles away, those proposals will go out the window.

- Checklist of matters. Has the mother really thought this all through and made proper arrangements for the children? She must give convincing reasons for uprooting the children and her proposals must be realistic. What are her plans? Has she considered:

- Schooling. Availability? Suitability?

- School holidays. These may be completely different in the country she is moving to and contact could be limited on that basis alone.

- Child care arrangements if the mother is going to work full time.

- Housing. Availability? Suitability? Location?

- Her contact proposals. Realistic?

- Employment. Is she working and if so, what will she be doing?

- Language problems.

- Her new partner/husband. What is his relationship like with the children?
- Degree of commitment? How solid is the new relationship? What is his attitude? This may have an effect on the contact. The welfare of children is best served by being brought up in a happy, secure family atmosphere.

Consequently, if the mother's plans are ill-conceived, her application for leave will be refused, even if those plans are genuine. In one case the mother planned to relocate to Jamaica with her son and her maternal grandfather. The court refused her application because her plans were poorly thought through, there was no benefit to her son in relocating and the close bond with his father would most likely be severed as the father could not afford to fly out to Jamaica for contact. Furthermore, as Jamaica is a non-convention country, the father might have difficulties enforcing any order for contact.

The court might allow the mother to relocate but attach stiff conditions to the grant of leave such as requiring mirror orders to be obtained in the country to which she is relocating and appropriate undertakings from her so as to ensure contact takes place. She might for example be required to help with the cost of funding contact visits. In a recent case money from the sale of the mother's English property was held to the order of the court to provide the father with reassurances as to contact.

In one case where the mother was granted leave to remove the children to the USA and where the children had been dividing their time between the parents equally, the judge ordered that there was no reason why a joint residence order should not be made spanning both jurisdictions. On the basis the children would be spending significant amounts of time in both the UK and USA this was the appropriate order to be made. It is clear from this case that the court's decision depends very much upon the particular circumstances of the case before it.

Moving within the jurisdiction
There is another scenario where the mother does not emigrate but decides to move to the other end of the UK. At least in a situation where the mother is emigrating, the father has the opportunity to put his case when the mother makes her application for leave to remove the child from the UK. If she moves within the UK he does not have this opportunity. For example, a father might be further away or just as far away from his children in the UK than a father whose children are in Northern Europe, but can do very little about it. What is more, if he does not have the money to pay for the cost of travel to see them, the contact will be severely limited. Is there anything he can do?

If a father wants to oppose the move and there is a residence order in force he could apply to the court for a variation of the residence order, or in exceptional circumstances he could apply under the Children Act for the court to impose conditions on any existing order. In a truly exceptional case a condition restricting the mother's own planned move could be contemplated. What would be an exceptional case? Where the child for example has serious health problems. In one case the child had Down's Syndrome with a life-shortening heart condition and respiratory problems and the judge imposed a condition on the order.[13] The mother appealed. The Court of Appeal decided that a move might cause severe emotional difficulties for the child and impede the father's contact and that the judge in his discretion was right to impose the condition.

The fact that contact with the father will be adversely affected will not be enough to prevent the mother's move in itself. This is a circumstance where making a shared residence order might be appropriate – to maintain that crucial link between father and child.

---

13 Re S (A Child) Residence Order: Condition [2001] EWCA Civ 847 [2001] 3 FCR 154 Civ 1795 [2003] 1 FCR 134

Chapter 14
Contact

Reasonable contact

What is reasonable contact?

What one father may regard as reasonable contact may not be so to another father, but generally, whatever the level of contact, it is not enough. Unfortunately, there is no definition of reasonable contact in the 1989 Children Act, nor anywhere else for that matter. The Government asserts that it cannot be defined since 'every case is different' and therefore there cannot be any legislation on it because we do not have a consensus on what it is. This makes for dissatisfaction all round and it is very easy to see how the system may be abused by a resident parent who wishes to deny the child's ongoing relationship with the other parent. As matters currently stand a father would be regarded as having very reasonable contact if he had contact every other weekend, telephone contact during the week and a couple of weeks holiday contact in the Summer and the rest of the holiday time split, although not necessarily equally. We look at the proposals for reform in this area in Part III.

It goes without saying that when the parent's relationship breaks down it is important to minimize disruption to the children but if they have a loving relationship with their father then the benefits of that to them, and the continuity of contact with him, will far outweigh any negative aspects. The reality is that after separation children's routines are going to be disrupted anyway, as instead of having one base they will have two, a direct consequence of their parents splitting up. But the disruption can be limited by the parents and, at the end of the day, what is important is to build healthy relationships. If a father does not have a sufficient degree of contact once he and the mother part, it is harder to build up the relationship with his children and they lose out.

Those advising fathers against the backdrop of contested divorce and/or financial proceedings, often recommend the father to 'back–off' and not press the mother on contact issues until the whole situation simmers down. Fathers are therefore placed in the unenviable position of having to wait to resolve matters, which in turn can cause frustration and encourage conflict and resentment because, once again, this leaves him in a no-win situation and subject to the whims of the mother.

Existing approach

The starting point is that the child has a right to know both parents and should have contact with the non-resident parent who in the majority of cases will be his/her father. There is a normal assumption that a child will benefit from continued contact with this parent, but that assumption can always be displaced if the child's interests indicate otherwise. The welfare of the child will always be the paramount consideration. The court is only concerned with the parents' interests insofar as they affect the welfare of the child and will refer to the welfare checklist of seven factors we looked at in detail in Chapter 10.

The problem for a non-resident parent seeking contact is that the onus is always on him/her to prove that more contact would be in the best interests of the child, whereas the resident parent is not obliged to show why contact should not take place. Because of the 'every case is different' approach and because there is no clear guidance on how much contact to recommend, it follows that any outcome can flow from any facts and contact can be stopped for any reason. A 'fit' parent has no presumptive entitlement to any time with the children.

Further, where the contact has stopped and there has been a period of no contact, the test to be applied is whether there are any cogent reasons why the child should be denied the opportunity of contact with the non-resident parent. Before ruling out the establishment or re-establishment of contact the court will wish to be satisfied that all avenues have been tested, then there is the likelihood of protracted litigation, delay, CAFCASS reports, investigation of allegations of abuse, violence etc.

The form of contact

The court has a wide and comprehensive jurisdiction to make contact orders. It can order for direct contact or indirect contact to take place and can attach conditions to the contact.

Direct contact

This means seeing and being with the children – face to face contact. The amount of contact can either be specified in the order or the order could be for 'reasonable' contact in which case the arrangements can be made between the parents. However, this can be unsatisfactory because, as we looked at above, the definition of 'reasonable' is in itself unclear and can be abused by a mother wishing to be awkward.

Where there is an order for direct contact there has to be a positive obligation on the parent who is to allow contact to take place. This is important from the point of view of enforcing the order. The order should state that the mother 'must make the children available for contact' with the father rather than to say that he is 'to have contact with the children'. The difference between the two is that the former is enforceable, in principle at least if not in practice, and we look at this below.

There is no set format for the order. It depends upon the case. It may set out times and dates and there may be conditions attached to the contact or to enable contact to take place.

If a father has not seen his child for some time or, for example, in a situation where there has been domestic violence, the order may contain conditions and directions for the contact to be built up gradually. Depending on the circumstances of the case, the contact could be either supported or supervised.

There are several forms of supported contact. It might be that the other parent is present during the contact visit; a friend or other relative is present; or the contact takes place at a contact centre. Where the supported contact does take place at a contact centre several families are in the room at any one time. Staff and volunteers observe the contact sessions and only step in if a child becomes distressed or a person behaves inappropriately.

Where the contact is to be supervised it will probably take place at a local contact centre. Only one family will be present in the room at any one time and the person who monitors contact will observe it closely. Generally, supervised contact is only available if a fee is paid or if a family is referred to the centre by Social Services or CAFCASS and so this is dependent on available resources.

Where contact is ordered to take place at a contact centre there must be a contact referral which has to be delivered to the contact centre by the Applicant's solicitor. The National Association of Child Contact Centres (NACC) has a protocol for referrals.

Indirect contact

This could be by telephone calls, letters, cards, e-mails, photographs, audiotapes, or videos for example. There might be a direction that the absent father should be sent school progress reports and any cards or letters he sends to the child be read to the child. An order of this nature would stipulate that the mother was to allow the father to have indirect contact with the child. Indirect contact can be used as a way of re-introducing a child to someone he/she does not know very well or at all, but unfortunately all too often indirect contact can be easily eroded by the resident parent.

In one case the father was American and his wife was English but was working in America where they met. They married, and moved to the UK and had a daughter. The relationship broke down when their daughter was eighteen months old. The mother remained in the UK and went to live with her parents; the father's employment contract came to an end and he returned to the USA to work. The end of the relationship was very acrimonious and the mother and her family were hostile to contact and determined to limit contact as much as possible.

The father only had two weeks holiday a year and tried to organize his flights to the UK so that he would come over on a Friday and return home on a Monday, thereby carving out ten contact visits a year. He would book his flights well in advance and agree the dates with the mother but the mother would change the arrangements at the last minute. When he did see his daughter he had to go to her parents' house, was never left alone with her, the argument being that he was 'a stranger' to her as she had been so tiny when the parties had separated. The opportunity to develop a meaningful father/daughter relationship was denied. The problem was ongoing.

When the matter came to a head and the father made an application to the court the daughter was aged three. The father explained his predicament and how his attempts to see his daughter were constantly being thwarted by the mother. The District Judge said that the child was very young and that the father should send her a card on her Birthday and that he could telephone his daughter even though it was evident to everyone that it was unlikely he would ever manage to speak with his daughter. The father was devastated. He indicated that, at the hearing, the District Judge was not interested in listening to his arguments about how hostile the mother was to contact, but took pains to accommodate her at every level and accepted her 'reasons' for limiting the contact. Unsurprisingly, he went away with no confidence in the system whatsoever.

Attaching conditions to contact

We looked at making the contact conditional upon it being supported or supervised above. Where there is indirect contact we also looked at the fact that the court can make a direction for the resident parent to provide the person having contact with progress reports and photos. There are other conditions which the court may attach to the order. For example:

- Relating to the 'pick-up' and return of the child.
- Travel costs.
- Method of transportation.
- Where the child may go or who the child may see during contact visits.
- That the party with contact does not drink alcohol during the contact visit.

The Children & Adoption Act 2006, which we look at in detail below under enforcement of contact, gives the court power to attach a contact activity condition, requiring a person who has been granted contact to attend a specified contact activity.

What happens where there has been domestic violence?

Where there has been a history of domestic violence between the parents this will impact on the court's decision on the level of contact granted. This is the case even though the child has not been physically harmed. For example, it may be that after the parties split the mother argues she is concerned that on contact visits the father might be violent towards the children. Furthermore, she may also be afraid that he may be violent towards her again if she is not compliant over contact. Domestic violence is one of the most common reasons why a mother refuses to comply with a contact order.

On 12 April 2000 the Lord Chancellor's Department issued a Report on the issue of contact between children and violent parents. It set out proposed Good Practice Guidelines for courts dealing with cases in which domestic violence is raised as a reason for the refusal of contact or for that contact to be limited. The Government accepted the Guidelines. The Report was based upon the responses to a Consultation Paper issued the previous year. The definition of 'domestic violence' used by the Paper covered physical, sexual or emotional abuse.

Although there is no presumption against contact, where domestic violence is proven to have taken place, the court has historically exercised its discretion as to the level of contact awarded. The court has always considered negative factors. These are the seriousness of the violence, the risks involved, the impact on the child (that is the effect that exposure to domestic violence between the parents has had on the child), the impact on the residential parent and the motivation of the parent seeking contact. These negative factors have been balanced against positive factors and consideration given to the recognition by the violent parent of past conduct and that parent's commitment to change.

Under the Guidelines, where there has been a finding of domestic violence the court is recommended to consider all the above. Careful consideration has to be given to the motivation of the parent pursuing contact. Does the parent genuinely believe it is in the best interests of the child for contact to take place, or is it just a way to continue the campaign of harassment, intimidation or violence against the other parent?

Having made an order that there should be contact even though domestic violence has taken place, the court then has to decide on the form of contact. For example, the court may decide that direct contact is in the best interests of the child but that it should be supervised. Conditions may be attached to the order. If a father is violent because he is an alcoholic, one of the conditions may be that he seeks treatment for his alcoholism. Contact may be for a set period and a date given for the order to be reassessed.

The Guidelines state that on an application for interim contact where the allegations of domestic violence have not been decided upon as yet, the court should give particular consideration to the likely risk of harm to the child. This applies whether contact is granted or refused. The court should ensure, so far as it can, that any risk of harm to the child is minimized and that the safety of the child and the residential parent is secured before, during and after any such contact.

The Adoption & Children Act 2002 amended the Children Act to include the recognition of the harm that children can suffer by actually witnessing domestic violence. As we saw in Chapter 10, in all cases where the court considers the welfare checklist the court will have to decide if domestic abuse, violence or harm has taken place and, if so, what the likely harm is to the child at the present time and in the future. Harm is now defined as including impairment from seeing or hearing the ill-treatment of another. We also looked at form C1A in Chapter 10 and how the court investigates allegations of violence and abuse.

The Court of Appeal has confirmed that in every case where domestic violence is put forward as a reason for refusing or limiting contact, the court should consider the allegations made at the earliest opportunity, and decide whether the nature and effect of the alleged violence is such as to make it likely that the order of the court for contact will be affected if the allegations are proved.[14] The earliest opportunity for the court to consider the matter will generally be at the First Hearing Dispute Resolution Appointment (FHDRA).

Where there has been child abuse, individual circumstances should be taken into consideration, and if there is documented proof of abuse or irresponsible behaviour, the courts should be free to make their decisions accordingly. It is a sad fact that each year thousands of fathers are falsely accused of child abuse. Mothers use this as a means by which contact can be prevented. However, proof of the child abuse must be shown. The problem is that it is all too easy to make allegations and once allegations have been raised the court must err on the side

---

14 Re H (Contact: Domestic violence) 2005 EWCA Civ 1404

of caution and investigate them fully. Time wasted on cases where false allegations are made means less time devoted to genuine cases where children really need protection. That needs to be borne in mind in light of a report by Women's Aid on child homicide during contact, *Twenty nine child homicides* (2005).

The whole issue of domestic violence has been a driving force in relation to the Government's proposals for reform on the issue of contact. In the Green Paper – *Parental Separation: Children's Needs and Parent's Responsibilities* the Government states that it 'firmly believes both parents should have responsibility for and a meaningful relationship with their children after parental separation – with the important proviso that it is safe'. In relation to the courts it states 'that the general principle to be applied by the courts is that both parents have equal status as parents and that the courts expectation is that both parents should continue to have a meaningful relationship with the chidren following separation, as long as it is safe and in the child's best interest.' The problem with the 'as long as it is safe' proviso is that it can be exploited – at present there is nothing to secure the children's right to parenting time when it is being obstructed without there being any safety issue at all.

Domestic violence does not affect only women and children, but also men and the issue of violence against men is often swept under the carpet.

Interim contact

An interim contact order might be made pending agreement or a final order. The court's approach depends on whether the dispute is about:

- Contact taking place at all, or
- How frequently or where it should happen.

If the dispute relates to contact taking place at all, interim contact will be ordered only if the court feels contact must take place so that the contact can be observed or assessed by a CAFCASS officer or other expert, or if the judge has heard enough evidence to decide whether interim contact is in the child's best interests.

If the dispute relates to the frequency and/or place of contact, then the court may try to decide what interim contact should take place without investigating all the evidence.

No contact at all

A contact order can also be made preventing contact with someone. Another way of achieving this is to obtain a prohibited steps order, and we look at this in more detail in the next chapter.

In deciding whether contact should cease or be reintroduced, the court will apply the principle that no court should deprive any child of contact to either parent unless it is wholly satisfied that it is in the interest of the child that contact should cease. This is a conclusion at which the court is extremely slow to arrive. It would be a very drastic order because, as we have seen, it is usually deemed in the best interests of a child to have contact with the father.

The court cannot make an order forcing someone to have contact with a child.

Varying a court order for contact

The parties can vary a court order any time by agreement. The order for contact could contain a clause 'and any such further contact as may be agreed between the parties.' A party generally makes an application to the court to vary a contact order where he/she wants to change the contact arrangements and the other party will not agree.

Controlling further applications being made

The court has the power to make an order that no further applications may be made by a party without obtaining the permission of the court first. For example, where there is a history of a party making unreasonable applications the court might use this power – the party against whom the order is to be made should have the chance to put his/her case as to why the order should not be made. In practice the making of such an order does not prevent that party making further applications, but it means subsequent applications will be monitored by the court.

Enforcing contact

There are two aspects to this, and these are making an application to court for a contact order where the father's contact is limited and making an application to enforce the contact order. The Children & Adoption Act 2006 includes a range of proposals to monitor and enforce child contact orders and we look at these below. However, the primary difficulty is not in enforcing orders but in obtaining an order worth enforcing in the first place.

By making an application for a contact order

For some, once the order is made, that is sufficient and the parties do manage to comply with it even though their own relationship is still very strained. However, it may be necessary to make further applications if other issues arise or there are changes in circumstances and the parties cannot agree these between themselves.

By making an application to enforce the contact order

A father faces a predicament where he has obtained a contact order but the mother still refuses to allow contact to proceed. He probably applied for an order for contact in the first place because the mother was seriously sabotaging contact. Unfortunately, for some fathers the sabotage does not cease merely by the fact that a court order is in existence. These are situations where the mother is totally opposed to contact – implacable or hostile to contact.

Children & Adoption Act 2006

This Act provides the courts with new powers to promote and enforce contact orders as follows:

- Where there is a dispute about contact the court may direct a party to undertake a 'contact activity' first, that is before making an order at all. For example, to attend information sessions; meetings with a counsellor; parenting programmes or classes. Mediation is not included as a contact activity because the Government believes it must be entered voluntarily and so parties could not be directed by the court to attend mediation compulsorily – although the parties could be directed to attend a mediation session for the purpose of learning about the benefits of it.
- Similarly, on the making of the contact order the court will be able to attach conditions requiring a party to undertake a contact activity.
- The Act enables the court to require a CAFCASS officer (or a Welsh Family Proceedings Officer) to monitor a contact order, monitor contact activity and report to the court on compliance with the order concerned.
- Under the 1989 Children Act the court was able to make a family assistance order requiring a CAFCASS officer or Local Authority officer to advise, assist and generally help with the smooth running of the order, but the order could only be made in exceptional circumstances and run for six months. Under the Children & Adoption Act 2006 the exceptional circumstances requirement has been removed and the order extended to twelve months.
- Where a contact order has been breached the court has power to make an enforcement order imposing an unpaid work requirement such as community service; or to order one person to pay compensation to another where financial losses have been incurred as a result of the breach: for example, where the cost of a holiday has been lost.

Existing powers
The powers provided by the Children & Adoption Act 2006 are in addition to the courts existing powers as follows:

- If the court is satisfied that the mother has not given the child up for contact, it could make an order authorizing an Officer of the court or a constable to take charge of the child and deliver the child to the father. The whole scenario is very unsatisfactory from a practical point of view and could cause more harm than good for the child. This is why mothers who are determined to block contact are able to do so effectively, because judges are very reluctant to make an order which could be detrimental to a child.
- In the County Court and High Court the breaking of a court order is known as a 'contempt of court'. The penalty for this can be imprisonment, committal or a fine. For the contemnor's (that is the one in contempt) assets to be sequestrated – this means that they are frozen. Although freezing the assets can be useful where the contemnor has gone abroad, in child abduction cases the court is more likely to order committal. Before any committal order can be made the court has to be satisfied beyond reasonable doubt that the defendant knowingly broke the order. Furthermore, the requirement is that a penal notice must have been attached to the order in question. A penal notice is a notice informing the person against whom the order is made that a failure to obey it constitutes a contempt of court for which the offender may be sent to prison.

The courts regard these as remedies of last resort. These are provocative and emotional applications and could be very damaging. It is important not to lose sight of the child's welfare. If the mother is totally hostile to contact the court must look carefully at her reasons. Even if a mother is found to be unreasonably hostile, the courts are very unwilling to lock up mothers who refuse to comply with contact because of the impact this will have upon the child.

The whole area of enforcement of contact orders is highly contentious and the financial compensation provisions included in the Children & Adoption Act 2006, although well-meaning, are likely to be unsatisfactory as the resident parent, generally the mother, does not have the money to pay compensation. Where a contact dispute is intractable the children should be represented separately and we looked at this in Chapter 11. Further, although the transfer of residence is not to be used as a punishment for contempt, where it is justified on welfare grounds then the court should use its powers to transfer it.

Chapter 15
Emergency procedures

Prohibited steps order

We looked at the definition of a prohibited steps order in Chapter 6. The first point to note is that the court cannot make a prohibited steps order if the purpose behind it is to achieve a result that could be achieved by a residence or contact order. It is easier to demonstrate by example exactly what can be achieved by this order.

Where a prohibited steps order would be appropriate

- In an abduction case, if the father has abducted the child and the result required is for the abducted child to be returned to the mother, the correct order for her to seek is a residence order with appropriate conditions and directions preventing unauthorized removal.
- If the child is living with the mother and she abducts the child abroad and the required result is to obtain the return of the child to the UK and to prevent further removal of the child, then a prohibited steps order is the correct order to obtain. The child will nevertheless remain living with the mother.
- If no residence order were in force, a prohibited steps order could be used to prohibit the removal of the child from the country or prevent a change of surname. We looked at changes of name and removal from the jurisdiction in Chapter 13.
- If a father wants to obtain an order preventing a child from living with someone else, the correct order would be a residence order.
- A prohibited steps order could be used to prevent another party from registering or enrolling a child at school or from permitting or preventing a child from having medical treatment.
- Sometimes it is difficult to know which would be the most appropriate order and it really does depend on circumstances. In one case where the mother's cohabitee had abused the children, the court decided that a 'negative' contact order preventing the mother from allowing contact would only afford partial protection. The court made a prohibited steps order against the cohabitee instead.
- If an order is needed to restrict publicity, a prohibited steps order is not the appropriate order. This is because a prohibited steps order can only relate to matters which are included within parental responsibility and publicity is not one of these matters. This would be covered by the wider powers of wardship and dealt with by the High Court. We looked at this in Chapter 12.

Specific issue order

We looked briefly at specific issue orders in Chapter 6. A father would need to apply for a specific issue order where he disagrees with a decision the mother has made in relation to a specific issue and which they cannot resolve between themselves. In the same way as a prohibited steps order, a specific issue order cannot be used to achieve 'back door' residence or contact orders.

Where a specific issue order would be appropriate

The following are examples of specific issue orders:

- For the court to decide which school the child should attend because the parents cannot agree.
- For the court to decide whether the child should have a particular operation or course of treatment.
- The religion the child should adopt.
- If it is desired to prevent anyone having contact with the child, this seems to be the appropriate order to obtain as it is accepted that a contact order can only authorize contact and not prevent it. However, it has been held that the court could make a contact order providing for no contact. The person with whom the child lives could be prevented therefore from allowing contact with an abusing parent or someone else the court considered was harming the child in any way.

Child abduction

Basics

In Chapter 13 we looked at residence orders and the effect of a residence order where a party wants to take a child abroad as well as applications for leave to remove a child from the jurisdiction, but the important issue is when the removal of a child becomes an abduction matter.

Authorized removal or abduction?

- If a residence order is in force, it may have conditions attached to it about removing the child. The court can enforce the conditions by an order that the child be produced to the parent with the residence order.
- If there is no residence order in force, an ex parte application for a residence order or prohibited steps order could be applied for and then enforced by the court. The court has power to order anyone who may have information as to a child's whereabouts to disclose it to the court.
- If the child is removed from England to another part of the UK, this enables a s8 order to be recognized and enforced by a local court. The order has to be registered.

- If a mother has a residence order, the father will commit an offence if he does not have her consent or the permission of the court to remove the child. She will not commit an offence if she removes the child unless they are away for more than one month and it is clear they are not on their way back.
- Where there is no residence order in force and the father removes the child no offence is committed 'initially' but this will become a criminal offence if he refuses to return the child. In any event, it is a criminal offence for any person except a person with parental responsibility to take a child from any person without lawful authority or reasonable excuse.

Preventative measures

Port alert procedures

If there is an imminent threat of abduction (that is within the next 24 to 48 hours) then the port alert procedure can be used. The application should be made to the Applicant's local police station or, if it is urgent or a court order has just been made, to any police station. The authorities will need a full description of the child who is travelling, the likely abductor and time of travel, the place they are expected to leave from, probable destination, and photographs. Curiously enough, there is no need for a s8 order to have been obtained if the child is under 16 although if there is an order in existence it should be produced to the police. On the other hand, the system is only available for children over 16 if a s8 order exists.

The child's name will remain on the 'stop' list for four weeks and will then be removed unless another application is made to the police.

Passports

If a father wants an order preventing the issue/surrender of a passport, he can only obtain it if there is already in existence an order prohibiting or restricting the removal of the child from the UK – for example, a prohibited steps order forbidding removal; a residence order in his favour confirming that his consent is required to allow the removal to take place; an order confirming that the removal is contrary to the wishes of the court. As part of an order there may be a direction that the child's passport be lodged with the other party's solicitor if there is a threat of abduction.

If a child's details are registered with the passport agency so that no passport may be issued, it is important to remember that the registration is only effective for twelve months and therefore must be re-registered.

Remedies

Although a criminal offence will be committed if a child is abducted abroad, it will not bring about the return of the child. The Hague Convention of Civil Aspects of Child Abduction 1980 and the European Convention of Recognition and Enforcement of Decisions Concerning Custody of Children 1980 provide procedures for tracing a child and for his/her return. If the other party has taken the child to another country it may be possible to obtain the child's return, but this depends upon the country.

Convention countries

If the child has been removed unlawfully to a convention country without the other parent's consent and wrongfully retained there, the Convention will be able to help with the return of the child. The Hague Convention provides that the Central Authority of the country to which the child has been taken must help the parent find the child and protect the child once found. If a child is abducted, a parent must take immediate action and commence proceedings for the return of the child because after one year the return of the child becomes more difficult, although it does not mean that a return is impossible.

Where proceedings are commenced more than one year after the abduction, one of the issues the court will need to consider is whether the child is settled in his/her new environment. This does not just mean by virtue of the fact that the child has physically been there for over a year, but also from an emotional and psychological point of view. The more deceitful and sly the abduction, the more difficult it will be to establish emotional and psychological settlement. Even if it is established, the court has a residual discretion under Article 18 of the Convention to order the return of the child.

Non-convention countries

Where a child is abducted to a non-convention country, for example Saudi Arabia, then the court is free to determine the case on its merits under the wardship jurisdiction, although it will commonly have regard to the factors specified in the Hague Convention in reaching its decision. The court may make the child/children wards of court and order the abductor to return the children to the jurisdiction. If the abductor fails to do so, the court may make an order that the abductor is in contempt of court and can then make an order freezing the abductor's assets in the UK, that is sequestrate them. If the abductor returned to the UK he would then be arrested.

Other procedures

Missing children – Family Law Reform Act s33

Where a child is missing the court may make an order requiring any person whom the court has reason to believe has relevant information about the whereabouts of a child to disclose that information to the court. This means that the order may be directed to persons who are not parties to the proceedings. An order cannot be made unless there are proceedings to which s33 applies – for example proceedings for a s8 order or under the Child Abduction and Custody Act 1985. The application is made on form C4 and there must be a statement in support of the application. It should normally be made on notice but may be made ex-parte in an emergency.

Application for recovery of a child – Family Law Reform Act s34

Under s34 where a party has failed to comply with an order to give up a child, such as a s8 order for example, any court may authorise 'an officer of the court or a constable' physically to take charge of the child, with the use of such force as necessary, and for the delivery of the child to the person entitled. The order will not be made unless it is in the interests of the child and use of the order is more likely to be appropriate for transfer of residence than for achieving contact.

The application is made on form C3 with a statement in support of the application. As with applications under s33 it should normally be made on notice but may be made without notice in a case of emergency. What the court might do is make an 'unless' order which basically states that unless the party retaining the child hands over the child at a specified time and place, the power to take the child may be exercised. This allows that party to save face by delivering the child.

Chapter 16
Appeals

If deciding to lodge an appeal a father needs to know to which court to appeal, which rules cover that appeal, whether he has an automatic right to appeal or requires permission, how to prepare the case for appeal and what orders can be made. We look at the appeals process in family proceedings below.

Family Proceedings Court (FPC)

- Currently all appeals from the FPC are to the High Court.
- Permission to appeal is not required.
- The FPC has no power to grant a stay of the order, that is to stop the terms of the order being implemented, pending the appeal so it will be necessary to make any request for a stay to the High Court.
- The procedure is set out in the Family Proceedings rules 1991, rule 4.22. The notice of appeal has to be filed in the Principal Registry or the nearest district registry within 14 days of the date of the hearing. Within 14 days of receipt of the notice of appeal a Respondent's notice may be filed.
- As soon as possible after filing and serving the notice of appeal the Applicant must file and serve a paginated and indexed bundle – which should contain a certified copy of the application and the order, a copy of the notes of evidence, a copy of the magistrates' reasons for the decision and the reports and witness statements which were before the court; a summary of the hearing; a statement of issues; a chronology and skeleton arguments.

Current Developments

In Chapter 6 we looked at proposals to create a simple set of Family Procedure Rules. There are proposals to alter the process of appeal from FPC's to simplify it and for appeals to be made to a County Court instead of to the High Court.

County Court

Appeals

- A party may appeal against an order made or given by a District Judge to a circuit judge.
- Either the district judge who made the order or a circuit judge can stay the order pending the appeal.
- The procedure is set out in the Family Proceedings Rules 1991, rule 4.22. The

notice of appeal has to be filed at the court where the order was made and served within 14 days of the date of the hearing. The remaining procedure is the same as an appeal from the FPC.

Re-hearing or setting aside an order

If you believe that the judge has made an error regarding the law then the remedy is an appeal. But if, for example, there was a problem because information was withheld, then the judge might set aside the original order, make another order or rehear the case. The judge can consider new evidence which has come to light.

High Court

- A party may appeal against an order made by a District Judge of the High Court to a Judge of the High Court.
- The procedure is set out in the Family Proceedings Rules 1991, rule 4.22 and is the same as the appeal process in the County Court.

Appeals to the Court of Appeal

- A party may appeal against an order made by a judge of the County Court or the High Court to the Court of Appeal.
- Permission to appeal is required. If the first hearing was in the County Court or High Court either one of those courts could give permission to appeal, in which case it should be granted at the actual hearing, or the Court of Appeal could grant permission. For permission to be granted there has to be a real prospect of the appeal succeeding or there has to be some other compelling reason why it should be heard – for example, to prevent a serious miscarriage of justice as in a case of alleged child abuse where fresh medical evidence has come to light about the child's injuries. If the case has already been appealed to the County Court or High Court, in other words if this is the second appeal, then only the Court of Appeal can grant permission and it will not do so unless it considers the case raises an important point of principle or practice or there is some compelling reason for it to hear the case.
- Either the County Court or High Court or the Court of Appeal can stay the order pending appeal.
- The rules governing these appeals are the Civil Proceedings Rules 1998 Part 52 and PD 52.
- The person making the appeal, the Appellant, must file an Appellant's Notice in Form N161 at the Court of Appeal either within the time scale directed by the County Court or High Court or within 14 days of the decision against which he wishes to appeal. If leave to appeal is required this must be requested in the notice which must be served no later than 7 days after it is filed. The grounds of appeal need to be clearly stated. Judges should set out their reasons

for making decisions as failure to do so will breach Article 6 – right to a fair trial – under the Human Rights Act.

- A Respondent who seeks permission to appeal will be subject to the same time contraints as the Appellant.
- The Appellant needs to lodge a bundle of documents and include an additional copy of his notice for the court, one copy for each Respondent, a copy of his skeleton argument, a sealed copy of the order he is appealing, the order granting or refusing permission to appeal plus the reasons, witness statements in support of the appeal and, where the judgment was recorded, an approved transcript of it. If there is no recorded judgment then a copy of the written decision should be included and if there was an oral decision then an agreed note of the judgment which has been approved by the trial judge may be filed instead.

Orders which may be made

When allowing an appeal the court can make a fresh order; decide that the case should be remitted for a rehearing to the original court which heard the case; or decide that the case should be remitted to a higher court.

Chapter 17
Other considerations....

Child Support

The road to hell is paved with good intentions – Child Support Act 1991

The intention behind The Child Support Act 1991 was that it would benefit children by ensuring they would receive maintenance from the absent parent, usually their father. The Child Support Agency (CSA) was set up in 1993 and the whole idea was that from then on the agency, rather than the courts, would deal with child maintenance. There were major problems because the formula for calculating maintenance was too complicated and the Agency was unable to deal with the backlog of claims and reviews of claims because the whole process was cumbersome. The result of this was that children did not benefit. In fact, statistics show that only one in five children derived some benefit from the Agency so the Act did not deliver what was intended.

The Child Support Pensions and Social Security Act 2000 was passed to make the whole area of child maintenance easier to understand, more accessible and easier to enforce so that there would be more money for the children. From 3 March 2003 a new way of calculating child maintenance was introduced. Unfortunately, the changes have done nothing to improve the collection of child maintenance, the CSA has failed to deliver and further reform is now crucial. It is proposed that the CSA be replaced with a more effective model and we look at this below.

The existing formula

The maintenance a non-resident father pays for any relevant children is calculated as a percentage of his net income. There are four rates of pay.

The rates of pay
- Basic rate: This applies to a non-resident father with a net weekly income of between £200 and £2,000. The percentage of net income is 15% for one child, 20% for two children rising to a maximum of 25% for three children or more. The resident parent can apply to the court for a top-up maintenance order in certain circumstances. For example, where there are additional educational expenses or the child is disabled.
- Reduced rate: This applies to a non-resident father with a net weekly income over £100 but under £200. He will pay £5 per week on the first £100 of his net income and a percentage of his net weekly income over £100. The percentages used to calculate the maintenance are different from the basic rate ones.

- Flat rate: This applies to a non-resident father with a net weekly income of £100 or less, or who is on benefits. The flat rate is £5, irrespective of the number of children.
- Nil rate: This applies to a non-resident father who is any of the following: a full time student; aged 16 to 19 and studying full time for A levels or NVQ level 3; a prisoner; living in a residential home or nursing home and receiving assistance for those costs.

Calculation of net income
What is taken into account and what is not?

- Tax, National Insurance and pension contributions will be deducted from a non-resident father's gross income.
- No deduction is made for a non-resident father's housing costs, even if a large proportion of his income is paid towards those costs!
- If he has investment income that will be included in calculating his net income.
- Deductions are made from the non-resident father's income for relevant 'other' children. A relevant other child includes his natural child from another relationship. It also includes a stepchild. It is sufficient that the child is a member of his household and that he or his new partner receives child benefit. The percentage deducted depends upon the number of relevant other children the non-resident father has and whether he pays under the basic rate or reduced rate, as this will alter the percentage to be deducted. The CSA maintenance calculation will be a percentage of what is left of his income after all deductions have been made.
- What about those who appear to have no/a limited income? A non-resident father will be given a deemed income if it can be shown that his lifestyle exceeds his professed income and that he ought to pay higher maintenance. An example would be someone who deals a lot in cash and does not declare his true income.
- The mother's income is ignored under the formula.
- There are a number of variations that can be made to increase or reduce the maintenance. For example, if a non-resident father pays boarding school fees for the relevant children that would be a ground for a variation.

Shared care
Maintenance is scaled down according to the amount of time the children spend with the non-resident father. The more the children stay with him, the less maintenance he pays as follows:

Number of nights	Fraction to subtract
52 to 103	One-seventh
104 to 155	Two- sevenths
156 to 174	Three-seventh
175 or more	One-half

There might be a situation where the non-resident father has qualifying children to stay for a different number of days. Here he would add up the total number of days for all the children who stay with him and divide by the number of children. For example, if child A stays 104 nights and child B 104 nights the scaling down is 2/7th and 2/7th divided by 2 = 2/14ths.

If the one-half threshold is reached for any given child, that is they stay with him for 175 days or more, then the maintenance is reduced by a further £7.

Current developments – a new Child Support Regime

On 13 December 2006 the Government published a White Paper: *A New System of Child Maintenance* setting out its proposals for reform.

- The existing CSA is to be replaced by the Child Maintenance and Enforcement Commission (C-MEC). The emphasis of the C-MEC will be on encouraging parents to make their own arrangements and to take financial responsibility for their children, but is to be backed up by a tough enforcement regime. It is proposed that enforcement powers include curfews and removal of passports for non-paying parties.
- In addition to more stringent enforcement procedures it is also proposed that it should be a requirement for both parents' names to be registered following the birth of their child, unless unreasonable to do so. Clearly the idea behind this is to track down the non-resident party more easily and to put the responsibility for maintaining children back on to that party rather than the state. It will be interesting to see how this proposal will be received especially as it has implications with regard to parental responsibility and paternity, both of which we looked at in detail in Chapter 8.
- There will be no immediate changes as the C-MEC will not be fully operational until 2010 and it is estimated that it will take about three years to transfer all cases into the new system. In the meantime the CSA will continue to operate until late 2008 while the new organisation is being set up.
- Legislation will be introduced in 2007/8 to end the current requirement that all lone parents who are receiving benefits must also submit a claim to the CSA to receive child maintenance. This will enable them to make a private arrangement for child maintenance. From 2008 parents with care claiming benefit can keep the first £10 per week of maintenance before it affects their benefits. From 2010 the plan is to increase significantly the amount of maintenance that the parent with care on benefit can keep before it affects the level of benefits they receive.
- In terms of assessing the maintenance to be paid, the starting point will be the paying party's latest tax year information which will be used to work out how much child maintenance should be paid; and the income used to assess the maintenance will be updated on an annual basis. Currently the whole process can be severely delayed and prejudiced by the non-resident parent not providing accurate income details or any income details at all. The idea is to prevent this happening.
- It is also proposed to assess maintenance on gross weekly income (that is before any deductions have been made) rather then net income. This is a rather worrying development for the non-resident parent and needs to be reviewed.

- The flat rate of maintenance paid by the bulk of non-resident parents on benefits will be increased from £5 to £7 per week once the future scheme has been implemented.

Many lawyers believe that where cases are complicated the CSA should not deal with them at all and let the courts do so. In this way resources would not be taken up by dealing with matters which are more appropriately dealt with by the courts and thereby reduce delay for other cases falling within the remit of the CSA.

Contact & Child Support

It has long been held that contact cannot be made conditional on the payment of maintenance but the fact is where there are outstanding child support issues they do have a bearing on contact. There are also many fathers who do pay maintenance and are still refused regular contact with their children. Where a non-resident parent has paid child maintenance regularly the courts should take this into consideration when dealing with enforcing a child's right to see both of his/her parents.

The Human Rights Act 1998 & The Children Act 1989

Implications of the Human Rights Act for fathers

The Human Rights Act does not provide more rights for a father, but it should provide easier access to those rights. The Act came into force on 2 October 2000 and incorporates into British law 'most' of the provisions of the European Convention on Human Rights (the Convention). The rights we have implemented are called 'convention rights'. This should not to be confused with the Hague Convention.

If a father makes an application under the Children Act what effect does the Human Rights Act have on the court's decision?

Whenever a UK court is considering the existing law, it has to look at that law and see whether it fits in with Convention rights. The law must be read in a way compatible with Convention rights, so if the court finds that a particular Act of Parliament does not fit with Convention rights what can the court do?

The court can only make what is called a 'declaration of incompatibility' because the Human Rights Act does not allow the courts to overrule an Act of Parliament. It is only the higher courts that will be able to make declarations of incompatibility, so in a family case if a query arises in the Family Proceedings Court or County Court, the case should be transferred to the High Court. The Government and Parliament have to decide if the law should be changed.

The Children Act was drafted with the intention that it would be compatible with the Act. The courts must read and give effect to children legislation in a way which is compatible with the Convention rights, so far as it is possible to do so, and it will be necessary for the courts to evaluate the effect of the legislation in particular cases to ensure compatibility.

It is not explicitly stated in the Convention that the children's interests are the paramount consideration, and the European Court, in interpreting the right to family life, has stated that the rights and freedoms of all concerned must be taken into account and a fair balance struck. The European Court has found that the best interests of a child may be the paramount factor in determining custody. The Commission has also said that the child's interests are dominant if there is conflict between the parent and child, in which event the interests of the child prevail. The European courts have not clearly indicated what factors the domestic courts should take into account in determining what is in the best interests of the child, but have indicated the importance of the continuity of development or consistency in the upbringing of a child.

Bringing a claim

Can a father bring a claim?

The Human Rights Act is like a code of conduct. This is set down in the form of Articles and Protocols. It is not a series of dos and don'ts. If a father wants to take somebody to court under the Act, he needs to show that the code of conduct has been breached. In legal terms this means he is a person who is a 'victim' of a breach of Convention rights.

Who are victims and how does a victim bring a claim?

A victim is a person. This includes an individual or a company, because in law a company is a legal person. The breach could be due to action taken, or failure to take action. The father need not have suffered harm because of the breach, provided there is a risk of him being directly affected. He could bring a claim if his family is at risk of being broken up by a particular policy, even if this has not occurred; for example, against a local authority that has made an application to take his child into care although the application has not yet been heard in court.

Who can a claim be brought against?

Public authorities alone have a duty to comply with the Convention, not individuals. In a contact case it is not possible for the father to complain that the mother is not respecting his right to family life by denying him the contact he desires. Public authorities include local authorities, the Police, and the Courts to ensure a fair hearing.

Which convention rights affect Family law and fathers' rights?

Article 6: the right to a fair trial

Just because a father does not succeed in his case, it does not mean that he did not have a fair trial – but everybody has a right to a fair trial. Each party must have a reasonable opportunity to present his/her case, including evidence, under conditions that do not place either of them at a disadvantage to the other party:

- Cases must be brought within a reasonable time. Delays where cases are not listed for lack of court resources will be unacceptable under the Convention and have been held to be a violation of it, but delays in other European jurisdictions are such that some UK delays may not seem that unreasonable. However, in relation to children, especially where a child has been removed from his/her parents, or contact has been stopped pending the final court hearing, delay is crucial and here there is a very real prospect that Article 6 could be breached.
- There must be an independent judge.
- Everyone is entitled to a public hearing and for the judge's decision to be pronounced in public. However, there are circumstances when a public hearing would not be appropriate, such as cases involving children. The proceedings are in chambers, that is, behind closed doors, and not open court. We looked at proposals for change in this area in Chapter 12.
- There is a right to know the judge's reasons for the decision.

Article 6 will be broken if these standards have not been met. Article 6 covers criminal and civil proceedings. Civil proceedings that are covered by Article 6 include disputes about with whom the children of separated parents should live, so Article 6 will be relevant in relation to contact disputes.

Article 8: the right to respect for private and family life

Respect for private life
There is no firm definition but it covers:

- The right for a person to get on with his own life without interference.
- The right to develop his personality and to form friendships and relationships with other people.
- The right to enjoy his sexuality.
- The right to control his body.

Respect for family life
This does not allow persons to claim a right to establish family life. It is a question of fact, taking into account all the circumstances. Some examples of family life are as follows:

- A married couple with children. A child born to married parents will be part of that relationship from the moment he/she is born.
- An unmarried father who cohabits with the mother and the children.
- Where the parties do not cohabit but the unmarried father has regular contact with his child and a strong bond, showing that there are family ties. He should show commitment, although where an unmarried father had not had regular contact with his child, family life has been found.
- A single mother and child.
- Family life has been held to exist where there is no blood link or legal link through adoption or marriage.
- Family life goes beyond the traditional family and may be established

between children and individuals not necessarily their parents to the extended family life.

- When parents divorce or separate their relationship ceases to be family life within the meaning of Article 8, but the relationship between parent and child may survive as family life. Contact is relevant here.
- It has been held to include a right for parents to insist measures are taken by public authorities to re-unite them with their children. Local authorities run particular risks in relation to contravention of the Convention with regard to children in care. The right of parents to maintain relationships with their children can be violated by termination of contact and placing for adoption.
- The right to information has been considered to be an aspect of family life protected by Article 8 in relation to records kept by a local authority for a child in their care.

What would be a justifiable interference into family life?

Article 8 is not an absolute right but a qualified one. This means that a public authority can break the right in certain circumstances so that it can intervene, but the public authority will have to show that it had a sound legal reason for doing so and that it was reasonable in all the circumstances of the case.

There is a balancing exercise between a court respecting an individual's right to his private life, and welfare of children. In cases where a court declines to make a contact order, particularly in implacable hostility cases, the Court will have to justify the decision that in the interests of the child the refusal was justifiable.

Cultural and religious practises have to be considered carefully as failure to respect them could result in the court and local authorities being in breach. An example of this is a case where the parties were Moroccan. When the parties were together, the whole family slept in the same bed. After separation the father continued to sleep with the children on contact visits in the same bed. A Child Welfare Officer reporting on this case felt that there was something 'suspect' about the behaviour and referred to it in an extremely derogatory way.

Care proceedings 'proper' will invite questions over family life and its disruption. Interference cannot be justified just because another family might simply provide a better home for the child. The aim of care proceedings will usually be to reunite the family as soon as possible.

Article 9: freedom of thought, conscience and religion

The right to bring up children in the religion of their parental choice is usually accepted as a parental right, but this can be a difficult area and it can be complicated. This is particularly so where both parents are of different religions and when they have separated there is a tug of war over the religion of the child. There may be applications within the Children Act.

Article 14: prohibition of discrimination

Parental responsibility is an area where unmarried fathers have been seen as discriminated against. The discrimination has been deemed justified by the court to protect the interests of the child and mother.

Changing a decision

If a party wants to change a decision that has been made by a public authority or for the court to order a public authority to do something, or stop doing something, he can apply for a procedure called a judicial review. A judge will review the case and decide if the public authority has acted unlawfully. He has three months from the decision or action he is challenging in which to take this step.

Compensation

If a party wants compensation as a result of a breach of his rights he can bring a claim for damages. He has one year from the date of breach to bring his case. The Court of Appeal has held that an action for damages should only be brought as a last resort, after all other avenues have been exhausted.

Just because there has been a breach of his rights does not mean that he will receive damages because they are awarded at the discretion of the court when it is 'just and appropriate' and 'necessary'. The level of any award should aim to achieve 'just satisfaction' rather than placing the claimant in the position he would have been in had the basis of the complaint not occurred.

Declarations of incompatibility

As we saw above, if the courts decide that a particular act does not fit with Convention law, all they can do is to declare it incompatible but they cannot overrule it. Only Parliament can do that.

Contact & The Human Rights Act

A number of fathers have relied on Article 8 to argue that they have a right to contact with their children and that a refusal to order contact would amount to a breach of their rights. One father managed to show that there had been a breach of his rights under Article 6, successfully arguing that delays in the court system meant that he had waited over two years for the final hearing of his contact application.

The Human Rights Act has not had a major influence on the decisions made in the majority of contact cases. This is because the Children Act focuses on the welfare of the child, whereas the Human Rights Act requires the court to balance the rights of all those parties concerned. This means that in a contact case, even if the court concludes that the adult person seeking contact has a relationship which comes within Article 8, after weighing up the competing rights of that person and the child, it still has the power to refuse or limit that contact. This is on the basis that on balance interfering with the rights of that person are justified because the rights of the child require it.

Chapter 18
Pressure for Change

Over recent years there has been been ever increasing pressure from relevant legal bodies, interested organizations including fathers' rights groups and individuals for the issue of post-separation contact to be addressed, and for the introduction of effective measures to achieve it. If a father shows a genuine commitment to his children and has the capability and capacity to look after them and there are no safety issues, then his involvement should be encouraged and facilitated. Why is it then that there are so many cases where that simply does not happen? In Chapter 14 we looked at the existing approach to contact and how easy it is for a hostile resident parent to ensure that the child's contact with the non-resident parent does not take place. We also touched on proposals for reform and pressure to introduce legislation so that when a relationship breaks down the children have a right to equal contact with both parents. We now look at the background to, and proposals for, reform in detail.

Proposals for Reform

Consultation papers

The 1998 Consultation Paper *Supporting Families* produced by the Government (and to which we have referred in Chapter 1) stressed the importance of fathers which was at least a positive start. In 1999 the Children Act Sub-Committee of the Lord Chancellor's Advisory Board on Family Law issued a consultation paper on the issue of contact between children and violent parents and produced its report in 2000 setting out recommendations for contact where there has been domestic violence. It is quite clear that the Government's approach to reform in the area of contact has been dictated and driven by research into domestic violence, hence amendments introduced by s120 of the Adoption & Children Act 2002 and the Government's concern to promote contact where it is safe. Certainly, it was after the Sub-Committee produced its report on contact and domestic violence that it then decided to consider the wider issue of contact. A further consultation paper *Making Contact Work* was published in 2001 followed by the Report *Making Contact Work* in 2002.

Making Contact Work highlighted:

- Dissatisfaction with the current legal system.
- That contact issues need to be addressed by means other than court proceedings.
- That the court process would continue to retain a role in intractable cases and that procedures would have to be improved to be more effective.
- That new legislation relating to enforcement would be required to provide the court with a range of remedies in intransigent contact cases where the court order is not being obeyed.

The July 2004 Green Paper *Parental Separation: Children's Needs and Parent's Responsibilities* included a number of proposals supposed to assist the facilitation of the 'meaningful relationship' parents should have with their children post-separation 'where it is safe', and to help divert parties away from the adversarial court process. These included proposals in relation to collaborative law, mediation, protection of children from harm, case management (earlier listing of hearings, reducing delay, judicial continuity etc), post-order follow up, use of family assistance orders to facilitate contact, and enforcement along the lines of the *Making Contact Work* report.

As part of its aim to divert parties away from the adversarial court process the Government proposed the Family Resolution Pilot Project (FRPP). The plan was to provide information to parents at the start of proceedings about, inter alia, the negative impact of parental conflict on children, workshops on conflict management and a planning session where they would be given examples of parenting sessions that work. FRPP did not proceed beyond the Pilot stage but, in my view, it was flawed from the outset because it started from the premise that the welfare of the child is best promoted by quality of contact between the child and the non-resident parent rather than quantity. Contact is about time and for a child to maintain and/or build a quality relationship with the non-resident parent he/she needs exactly that.

At the beginning of a case when an application is made to the court, to offer the best possible chance of settlement, it is crucial that firm guidance is given to the parties:

- On how much contact the court is likely to order if they cannot agree.
- That frequent and continuous contact is in the child's interests.
- That there is a clear presumption that the child is going to have parenting time with both parents taking into account any safety issues etc.

We looked at the parenting plans the Government has developed in Chapter 10. These can only be of limited benefit because they provide no guidelines as to how much time the child should spend with each parent, offer the parents no clear direction as to the judicial approach which would be taken if the matter proceeds to court and thus no incentive for a recalcitrant parent to settle. We consider the arguments in the next section.

The Government produced its report Next Steps in January 2005 setting out its agenda for reform as follows:

- It would not legislate to introduce a legal presumption of reasonable contact or of shared care. The Government was not persuaded that any legislative change would benefit children. We looked at the whole issue of contact in detail in Chapter 14.
- Legislation would be introduced for the facilitation and enforcement of contact including a greater role for family assistance orders, hence the introduction of the Adoption & Children Act 2006 which we also looked at in Chapter 14.
- It set out a series of steps to deal with the issue of the impact of domestic violence in contact disputes – we looked at the risk assessments which CAFCASS needs to carry out at the beginning of a case where there is cause to suspect a child is at risk of harm in Chapter 10.
- The Government indicated that it would improve the quality and availability of information and advice to help families. We looked at the issue of compulsory mediation, the provision of a mediation helpline in Chapter 2. Although mediation would not be compulsory it would be encouraged and the Government would also look at other methods of resolving disputes. We consider mediation further below.
- CAFCASS should focus on dispute resolution. This would mean less priority given to writing welfare reports. The concern is whether CAFCASS is able to take on this role and whether there is sufficient funding available for all the duties CAFCASS is now supposed to perform. Bearing in mind past criticisms this is an onerous undertaking to put on CAFCASS.
- In terms of the court process itself there needs to be better case management and a reduction in delay. We looked at the incorporation of the Private Law Programme in Chapter 10.

Giving effect to the intentions of the Children Act 1989

The Children Act states that the welfare of the child shall be the paramount consideration and the Government has confirmed that it shall remain so. The intention of the Children Act is to encourage both parents to continue to share in their children's upbringing, even after separation and divorce, so this must mean by the children spending time with each parent – that is having contact with them. But how much time should that be? How much time is necessary to establish that 'meaningful relationship'? What apportionment of the child's time with each parent represents the child's best interest? By infrequent visits lasting a couple of hours? By a 50/50 split or a 30/70 split of the child's time? By overnight stays? By alternate weekends and holidays with around 100 nights contact per year or more or less? The argument against any definition of time is that 'every case is different' and so no generalization may be made.

Rejecting a legal presumption of equal contact

In its 2004 Green Paper the Government stated that it does not believe 'that an automatic 50:50 division of the child's time between two parents would be in the best interests of most children' and that the 'best arrangements for them will depend on a variety of issues particular to their circumstances: a one size formula will not work.' For these reasons it rejected a legal presumption of equal contact. When this point was considered by the Constitutional Affairs Committee Family Justice: the operation of the Family Courts in 2005, the Committee recommended the insertion of a statement into the welfare checklist 'indicating that courts should have regard to the importance of sustaining a relationship between the children and a non-residential parent.' With respect to the Committee this does not actually further the issue at all. We consider a way around this in the next chapter.

Rejection of bias towards fathers

We looked at the issue of bias earlier. The Government has rejected complaints of bias towards fathers. Some think that the courts bend over backwards to accommodate fathers and we are always provided with statistics that since in 99% of cases fathers obtain a contact order they do not have a raw deal. How much contact they obtain is a different matter. Under the current system the apportionment of time could be anything between 0% and 100% and the fact is that a resident parent with half a mind to it can very easily erode that contact. What can be done?

Chapter 19
A way forward?

Contact for 'fit' parents

Despite what we are told too many fit parents are still denied contact with their children. The knock on effect is that grandparents and members of the extended family are also denied contact with these children. That cannot be right. The child's time should be shared between both parents unless a parent poses a safety risk and this can only be achieved by introducing a legal presumption which provides that all fit parents will have substantial contact with their children.

The split does not have to be a 50:50 one at all and therefore the argument against introducing it on the basis that a 50:50 split is unworkable and not in the best interests of the majority of children no longer applies. The introduction of this legal presumption would reduce conflict because it comes with a guarantee of substantial contact for all fit parents.

The judiciary gave evidence to the Constitutional Affairs Committee Family Justice: the operation of the family courts that the only legal presumption we can have is that the child's welfare is the paramount consideration and that any other presumption would conflict with it. But if the child's welfare is the paramount consideration and it is in the best interests of the child to have a 'meaningful' relationship with both parents where it is safe, how can there be a conflict as one facilitates the other?

Other jurisdictions – lessons to be learned?

Across various States of the USA there are schemes to ensure that parents and children remain in contact post-separation and these were implemented years ago. In Florida, for example, there is an early intervention model which works on a three stage non-court process:

- Court issued information is given to the parties at the moment proceedings are issued. They are provided with a video focusing on what is best for the child and a leaflet setting out the court's expectations and guidelines on proper parenting after separation. Early Interventions hinges upon giving parents guidance before the case, on how much contact there should be and leads to the development of time-linked parenting plans which would set out norms of contact as a framework for negotiation.
- Parent education. A parent orientation class for potential litigants is the next stage.
- Contact-focused mediation. One-off mediation for those still struggling to agree which is compulsory. The compulsory mediation requirement has a direct bearing on cases settling.

So what happens to ensure that the safety of the child is addressed? When an application is made the case is immediately assessed to ascertain whether there are any concerns. If there are it will be taken out of the non-court process and placed into the court process. Because many more cases are kept out of court, the court's time is freed up and valuable judicial input can be given to the more urgent cases. In Florida they have trained court managers to assess the cases when they come in to recognize a case that needs to be fast-tracked in this way.

Without knowing what contact arrangement is likely to be in the child's interests for various categories of case, it is not possible to advise parents in advance how much contact they should allow. Time-linked parenting plans are open to infinite variation depending upon the facts of the case and deal with the problem that 'every case is different.' By reviewing the information given to them, attending the parent education class and resorting to mediation if necessary, parents are able to design a parenting plan which is in the best interests of the child.

If the court's expectations can be conveyed in advance that creates predictability. Under our current legal process parties do not have a clear indication of what level of contact the court expects them to agree until they are well-entrenched in the proceedings. I have dealt with cases where no amount of pleading from one party to the other to reach an agreement has worked, but where the judge has intervened and clearly directed that he will make a certain order if the parties do not agree, and by that direction he has promoted agreement. It is unfortunate that his intervention could not be earlier but that is down to the current process, not the judge. If we had judicially led/backed time-linked guidelines setting out what sort of outcome is appropriate if the parties were to litigate, and which are communicated to the parties at the time the application to the court is made, that would focus the parents' mind.

Rights for the children

And what about the children? Is it not their right to expect that all measures will be taken to ensure that post-separation they are able to maintain and/or build relationships with both their parents? Article 8 of the European Convention for Human Rights makes it clear that the natural link between a child and his/her parent is of fundamental importance.

What rights to children actually have? The Green Paper *Every Child Matters* contains no mention of children's rights and every reference to the word 'rights' except the one when the Act refers to the United Nations Committee on the Rights of the Child 1989 (UNCRC) was removed. S10 of the Children Act 2004 imposes a duty on all children's services to promote children's well-being, but contains no mention of promoting their rights. In *Every Child Matters* the Government stressed the importance of involving children and listening to their views and it is encouraging to note that there is now a move towards the voice of the child being heard on matters which concern that child's welfare and future. Children's needs must come first.

Final thoughts

For fathers it is not a question of taking the children away from their mothers, but about giving loving, caring and responsible fathers a proper chance to be as involved as possible with their children where they are genuinely devoted and committed to them. A court order can never be a substitute for a fair and agreed arrangement between two parents genuinely acting in their child's interests, so it is ever more crucial that a more effective system is in place to keep as many cases out of court as possible and which delivers a solution acceptable to both parents and in the best interests of the children.

The question to be asked therefore is how effective the measures the Government has implemented are in ensuring that such a result is achieved? The second question to ask is how effective the measures the Government has implemented are in ensuring that if cases do proceed to court they are dealt with more effectively? These are interesting questions because, as we have seen throughout the course of this book, the Government has produced consultation paper after consultation paper considering reforms in this area and yet there is still much dissatisfaction with the current family legal system.

The major problem with the current system is that it is very easy to abuse and simple for a hostile parent to raise allegations of domestic violence and/or abuse to prevent contact taking place. As we have also seen, there is no incentive for a recalcitrant resident parent, who is totally opposed to the other parent, to come to an agreement with the other party. Furthermore, even if the recalcitrant parent does form an agreement there is nothing to prevent that parent from subsequently sliding out of it for one reason or another, or for no reason whatsoever as is sometimes the case. This happens irrespective of whether there is a court order or not. Enforcement is a very grey area despite reforms. While, for example, it is meritorious for the Government to promote voluntary mediation, that in itself will do nothing to broker an agreement in such cases. We have looked at compulsory mediation and the arguments for and against it and also at the approach taken in other jursidictions when applications are made to the court.

Due to the fact that this is a highly emotive and contentious area, it is unreasonable to expect any Government to be able to introduce legislation which will deal with every single point that could possibly arise. There will always be parents who, despite what measures are introduced, will do their utmost to flout contact arrangements and attempts to enforce them. But, that does not mean that changes cannot be made to improve vastly our current system to end the misery that thousands of parents separated from their children are going through on a daily basis. We have looked at these proposed changes, particularly in the last two chapters – such as legislating to introduce a legal presumption that post separation and/or divorce the children will have substantial contact with both parents, where there are no safety issues.

I would like to leave you with these thoughts. In Chapter 1 I referred to the case of the father who committed suicide by setting fire to himself. He had not seen his daughter for nearly two years and she had not even reached the age of three. According to his mother the legal system let him down and he lost all hope.

Essentially, of course, it was his ex-partner who prevented contact taking place but the legal system allowed that to happen.

We are constantly told that only 10% of parties make an application to court and that in 99% of those cases contact orders are made – the level of contact achieved is debatable – and that in only 1% of cases does the Applicant fail to obtain a contact order. That is all right then some might say; but it is not all right. The father who committed suicide is part of that 1% statistic and there are surely many cases just like his. Changes to the legal system are now too late for him and in particular for his daughter, but reforms could be made which would make a difference to other fathers and their children, and that has to be worth something.

Appendix

Some useful contacts and addresses

Catholic Marriage Advisory Council
Clitheroe House
1 Blythe Mews
Blythe Road
London W14 0NW
tel (+44) (0) 20 7371 1341
e-mail info@marriagecare.org.uk

Child Abduction Unit
81 Chancery Lane
London WC2A 1DD
tel (+44) (0) 20 7911 7094/7047
enquiries (+44) (0) 20 7911 7127
fax (+44) (0) 20 7911 7248

Children & Family Court Advisory & Support Service (CAFCASS)
CAFCASS Headquarters
8th Floor
Wyndham House
189 Marsh Wall
London
E14 9SH
tel (+44) 20 7510 7000
fax (+44) 20 7510 7001
e-mail webenquiries@cafcass.gov.uk
www.cafcass.gov.uk

CAFCASS legal
Details as above.

The Child Support Agency
There are various offices
tel 08457 133133
email csa-nel@new100.dss.gsi.gov.uk
www.dss.gov.uk/csa
Herald House
tel (+44) (0) 20 79209491

The Collaborative Family Law Group (part of Resolution)
PO Box 302
Orpington
Kent BR8 QX
tel (+44) 1689 820 272
www.collablaw.org.uk

The Department for Constitutional Affairs
Selborne House
54-60 Victoria Street
London SW1E 6QW
tel (+44) 20 7210 8500
www.dca.gov.uk

Fathers websites
There are numerous websites for fathers. A couple of websites which contain links to sites for father are:
www.dads-uk.co.uk/resources.htm
www.coeffic.demon.co.uk/organiz.htm

Foreign & Commonwealth Office
Consular Department
Clive House
Petty France
London SW1H 9HD
tel (+44) (0) 20 7270 4017

International Social Services
Cranmer House
39 Brixton Road
London SW9 6DD
tel (+44) (0) 20 7735 8941
(if the child is abducted abroad they can make enquiries about his/her whereabouts)

Jewish Marriage Council
Head Office
23 Ravenshurst Avenue
London NW4 4EE
tel (+44) (0) 20 8203 6311
fax (+44) (0) 20 8203 8727
email info@jmc-uk.org
www.jmc-uk.org

The Law Society
Law Society Hall
113 Chancery Lane
London WC2A 1PL
tel (+44) (0) 20 7242 1222
fax (+44) (0) 20 7831 0344
email info.services@lawsociety.org.uk
www.lawsociety.org.uk

Office for the Supervision of Solicitors
Victoria Court
8 Dormer Place
Royal Leamington Spa
Warwickshire CV32 5AE
tel 0845 608 6565
www.oss.lawsociety.org.uk

Legal Assistance

National Association of Citizens Advice Bureau (CAB)s
www.nacab.org.uk
www.adviceguide.org.uk

Law Centres Federation
www.lawcentres.org.uk

Federation of Independent Advice Centres
www.fiac.org.uk

Legal Services Commission
Children & Family Services Division
4th Floor, 12 Roger Street
London WC1N 2JL
tel (+44) (0) 20 7759 1132
e-mail family@legalservices.gov.uk
(Community legal service direct 0845 345 4345)

The National Association of Child Contact Centres (NACC)
Minerva House
Spaniel Row
Nottingham NG1 6EP
tel 0845 4500 280
e-mail contact@naccc.org.uk
www.naccc.org.uk

National Family Mediation
9 Tavistock Place
London WC1H 9SN
tel (+44) (0) 20 7383 5993
fax (+44) (0) 20 7383 5994
email general@nfm.org.uk
www.nfm.u-net.com

The National Family and Parenting Institute
430 Highgate Studios
53-57 Highgate Road
London NW5 1TL
tel (+44) (0) 20 7424 3460
fax (+44) (0) 20 7485 3590
email info@nfpi.org
www.nfpi.org

The National Youth Advocacy Service (NYAS)
99-105 Argyle Street
Birkenhead
Wirral
Merseyside CH41 6AD
tel (+44) 151 649 8700
fax (+44) 151 649 8701
e-mail help@nyas.net
www.nyas.net

Principal Registry of the Family Division
The Divorce Registry
First Avenue House
42-49 High Holborn
London WC1V 6NP
tel (+44) (0) 20 7947 6000

Resolution (formerly SFLA)
PO Box 302
Orpington
Kent BR6 8QX
tel (+44) (0) 1689 850 227
fax (+44) (0) 1689 855 833

Reunite
National Council for Abducted Children
PO Box 7124
Leicester LE1 7XX
(+44) (0) 116 2556 234
e-mail reunite@dircon.co.uk

Royal Courts of Justice (High Court)
Strand
London WC2
tel (+44) (0) 20 7947 6000

UK College of Family Mediators (UKCFM)
24-32 Stephenson Way
London NW1 2HX
tel (+44) (0) 20 7391 9162
fax (+44) (0) 20 7391 9165
email info@ukcfm.co.uk
www.ukcfm.co.uk